RIDING
THE
WORLD

THE BIKER'S ROAD MAP
for a Seven-Continent Adventure

by Gregory Frazier

A Division of BowTie, Inc.
Irvine, California

Karla Austin, *Business Operations Manager*
Nick Clemente, *Special Consultant*
Jarelle S. Stein, *Editor*
Kendra Strey, *Assistant Editor*
Jill Dupont, *Production Coordinator*
Susan K. White, *Book Design*
Jim Fisher, *Cover Design*

Library of Congress Cataloging-in-Publication Data

Frazier, Gregory W., 1947-
Riding the world: a biker's guide to a seven continent adventure /
by Greg Frazier.
p. cm.
ISBN 1-931993-24-6
1. Motorcycling—Handbooks, manuals, etc. I. Title.

GV1059.5.F73 2005
796.7'5—dc22   2004017008

BowTie Press®
A Division of BowTie, Inc.
3 Burroughs
Irvine, California 92618

Printed and bound in Singapore
10 9 8 7 6 5 4 3 2 1

TABLE OF CONTENTS

CROSSING THE CRAZY WOMAN— SETTING OUT

Before I leave on a long ride, I take the advice of friend and global road warrior Dave Barr and spend one minute in solitude on my motorcycle with the engine shut off and my eyes closed, imagining where I will be and what I will see as I ride around the earth. It is a little like goal-setting, and it helps me focus on my adventure, the things I would like to learn along the way, and what I hope to have gained by the end. Several times that goal has involved a fish and a crazy woman.

Cutthroat trout are special fish. On the Big Horn River where I live, in the Big Horn Mountains of Montana, these fish are so special that even if a fisherman is lucky or smart enough to catch one, he cannot keep it. Crow Indians can, but we paid for that right when we agreed to give up nearly all of the state of Montana 125 years ago and to quit picking on the settlers as they stole our land. I have been trying to catch a certain cutthroat trout for several years. It lives in the depths of a vortex in the river where the water swirls in a 40-foot-wide pool, 20 feet deep at its center. Most of the time the trout slumbers so deep in the pool

World riding expert and inspiration Dave Barr pauses in his trek by motorcycle. He crossed Russia's frozen landscape in the winter of 1997 on his Harley-Davidson.

it cannot be seen. But just after dawn, or in the shadows of the Big Horns at dusk, I sometimes see it four or five feet below the surface of the current, stationary, as the vortex swirls around it.

I always recognize this trout because it has a deformed dorsal fin, probably the result of a narrow escape from a bear or a fight with another fish. The cutthroat and I have aged together over the years; I watched it grow from 10 inches long to more than 30 inches long. It doesn't eat when the sun is up; during daylight I have dangled everything from flies to worms in front of it, and all were ignored. Whether it is a male or female I don't know. What I do know is that it has become one smart monster.

The fish was there when I left on my second motorcycle ride around the world in 1997. I walked down to the river in predawn darkness to fish that "one last time" before I started off on a journey that would take me to the ends of the globe, as far as I could ride a motorcycle north and south around the world. I like to fish almost as much as I like moving through the wind on a motorcycle, chasing perfect roads, and I wanted to try my luck once more before I set off on a dedicated ride, during which there would be no fishing, only riding and staying alive.

The fish was small that morning, less than a foot long; but as the sun came up I could see its white, deformed fin slowly moving back and forth in the dark water. For nearly an hour, I tried to catch the fish. Nothing worked. Finally, it swam deeper under the current and was gone. A timely exit for the sun was up, and I needed to leave. I had to close up my house, get on my bike, and ride 500 miles north by sunset. There would be no fish for breakfast on the dawn of my last day home—and maybe not for many mornings to come. If my ride followed the proposed plan, I might not be back for four years.

Over the next months, I often thought about that fish. My thoughts focused on why I had not been able to catch it. Should I have used a different lure or fly? Maybe some high-tech stuff, perhaps synthetic glowing eggs that emit a fish gourmet smell? Or a jiggle worm made of plastic?

While I was riding around Alaska on the first leg of my journey, some fishermen heard of my failure to catch

My motorcycle lies in Alaskan waters in 2003, felled when a 40-pound King salmon migrating upstream "at speed" hit my front wheel. My bike stalled, and I didn't get my foot down in time. I should have applied for a Guinness World Record as the first rider to be knocked off his bike by a fish!

the cutthroat trout and offered me a few Yukon Jack fishing tips as well as some special "Alaska fish catchers." After reaching my northern goal, I turned around and headed south, riding back and forth across the backbone of the Rocky Mountains toward the other end of the earth in South America. Believing I had figured out how to catch the trout, I decided to make a detour from my planned route, and back to the Big Horn River I rode.

Soon another morning, the same fish (though bigger), but this time a different bait. Same result: once again, no fish in the frying pan. So much for Yukon Jack secrets and the Alaska fish catchers. Frustrated, I got back on my motorcycle and rode to the bottom of the earth, Ushuaia, Argentina.

Some time later, financial hardships brought my motorcycle trip around the world to a temporary halt. I had to return to the United States to sell some photos and magazine articles so I wouldn't be forced to eat sand and push my motorcycle as I passed through Africa. During that unscheduled stop, I again waded into the Big Horn River, at dawn and at dusk, this time armed with fishing ammunition from South America. I saw my prey twice, but each time it ignored my foreign offerings. Mr./Ms. cutthroat was not fooled by any of the Latino gizmos and, I suspect, laughed at my ongoing efforts to tempt it.

Fishless, I resumed my journey. As I rode south from the Big Horns to the airport in Denver, I crossed the Crazy Woman Creek. Whenever I pass this creek, I am either close to arriving home or just leaving it again; the water is the line between being back out on the road

Christmas 1997 finds me and some new friends collected at road's end, the National Park of Tierra del Fuego at the tip of South America. We traded travel tales, shared meals, and pledged to meet again, somewhere on the globe.

Contrary to appearances in this picture in Namibia, I didn't end up pushing my motorcycle across the continent when I ran short on funds during my third world ride.

or close to coming to the end of a long ride. This time I had a deep sense of unfinished business, a need to settle something. Not catching that fish was a nagging in my subconscious that detracted from what was ahead—the rest of my second ride around the globe.

I returned to my planned route with replenished funds and rode to the top of Norway, the North Cape, as far north as I could ride on the European continent. There I met Norwegian fishermen. They shared some novel ideas and techniques on how to land my elusive cutthroat back in Montana. We talked during summer nights as bright as daylight, nights filled with Laplander swill and fishing stories.

In the spring, after having survived riding through Africa, Asia, and then Los Angeles rush hour traffic, I crossed back over the Crazy Woman with the fish foremost in my mind. The first thing I did after unsealing my little house was to set the alarm clock for 3:30 a.m. I wanted to be standing in the river, on the fringes of the vortex as the sun came up. I thought Mr./Ms. Cutthroat was about to learn why sushi is so common in Japan. The Japanese had some pretty good techniques for landing fish, and a few had been passed on to this wandering motorcyclist as I traveled through their country.

Standing up to my armpits in 5 feet of cold water in the predawn hours is not pleasant. It is like riding a motorcycle through Germany in the November rain. I can do it, but only my love for the wider venture (riding or fishing) makes it bearable. In practical terms, I prefer riding in early winter rain to wading in a chilly river because in the rain it usually takes some time before the cold water finds my unit hiding under a layer of Gore-Tex or PVC. Not so in 5 feet of cold water on the Big Horn River when the sun has yet to rise above the tree line! When wading out to where I knew the fish was lurking, I

sometimes imagined it chuckled as I stifled a yelp of discomfort in my clinched fist. It probably thought, "Here comes the Indian eunuch again."

This time the fish was huge. It had obviously moved up the food chain from flies to fry. It was the same fish, I could tell by the twisted and bent dorsal fin, but it must have weighed nearly ten pounds by then. Either life had been so good that its belly was swollen or it was holding hundreds of eggs.

The Japanese may know Asian fish, but they do not know Mr./Ms. Cutthroat in the Big Horn River of Montana, USA. After an hour of resisting my best Rising Sun presentations, the fish made one full back-and-forth swish of its tail (by then the size of my hand) and slipped deeper into the dark pool and out of sight. I went back at dusk, only to see the Cutthroat trout rise just minutes before my shriveled unit and blue legs cried, "Enough!" I decided to quit trying to catch the fish for the time being.

A spray-painted Honda, mounted atop a platform much like a rural mailbox, decorates a roadside in Japan. I came across this unusual piece of motorcycling art while riding through the country.

Thousands of miles from Montana, large brightly colored fish swim beneath a waterfall in Taiwan. When I saw them during a roadside stop, I was reminded of a certain Cutthroat trout back home.

The summer of 2001 found me being pulled by several forces. One was money: I needed to fulfill some contractual writing obligations and pay bills. Another was love and lust: the love of what I do best, ride motorcycles, and my lust for more two-wheeled wandering. I had a map of the world on the wall, at eye level, next to my bed. At night, before I turned off the light, I found myself looking at places I had not been, such as Bhutan and Taiwan. I also looked at places where I enjoyed riding, such as the Alps of Austria, Italy, and Switzerland; the South Island of New Zealand; and parts of South America. Dreams of again riding up and down while crossing that map would often fill my sleeping hours.

Another force pulling on me that summer was more Indian, cosmic, or mystical. One journalist friend of mine in Germany calls it "Indian hocus-pocus" because he cannot understand or relate to the forces. Maybe I spend too much time making faces at religion, UFOs, and ying and yang to explain the calling of those forces. I refer to it as my Indian or wanderlust spirit.

I knew that at that point in life I should have been smoking a big Cuban cigar, swilling fine French wine, and watching the American stock market. I had a long-closed trunk filled with tailored suits and several diplomas to prove that I was trained to be doing those things. The fact that I was not made me wonder if there was something out there pulling me away from things that are ultimately bad for me. I concluded that had I been born 160 years ago, I would be pretty much the same inside, a wanderer chasing the sun. Instead of riding a motorcycle around the world, I would have been riding a horse around North America,

Sometimes called the Mother Road, the Stelvio Pass in Italy winds its way upward through the Alps. I have hunted the best roads on the globe and found most to be located in those mountains; I often dream of riding them again.

ducking U.S. Army bullets, and trying to figure out how to get across borders.

Late in the summer, I decided to accept an invitation from a friend for a motorcycle rendezvous in Katmandu, Nepal—nearly halfway around the globe from the Big Horn Mountains. The proposal was to make the rendezvous while I attempted a third motorcycle ride around the earth, doing it on several different bikes. One would be 50 years old, another designed more than 50 years earlier, and the third one an Autobahn screamer. I wanted to taste the continents on motorcycles manufactured on the lands I was crossing.

"I'll take a quick ride, for love and lust" was what I thought when I woke and saw Nepal on the map before my feet slid off the bed. My plan was to jump on a bike, go back to Brazil, then make a couple of fast runs up and down the European Alps, jump over to India, ride into Nepal, and make the rendezvous. Afterward, I'd hire a couple Sherpas and tell them to take me to a yeti. I wanted to capture the yeti in a few photographs and write a few yeti stories. I would then get back on a motorcycle, swing through Bangkok, then over to Taiwan, and finally, back to the United States, picking up fishing secrets along the way. I thought I might also stop back in Japan and let the sushi guys know what Mr./Ms. Cutthroat thought of their fishing secrets and gear. Another option was a side trip through New Zealand, where there were supposed to be some pretty good trout catchers who could help me with fishing tips.

This much I knew: come April or May, dawn would again find me nipple

deep in the icy water of the Big Horn River as the red rays of sunrise chased night west around the globe. In the meantime, I would have a ride around the globe to figure out what I was doing wrong, absorb new advice from Asian fish catchers, and wait for that cutthroat trout to lose its edge.

I also knew that if I did catch the fish, I would let it go. It had outgrown every frying pan I own and should be

left to roam the Big Horn River from the depths of its home in the vortex. It had earned freedom. In the meantime, I would hunt yeti, which I had a far better chance of catching than the Big Horn cutthroat trout.

On the morning of my departure, I sat on my motorcycle, eyes closed, thinking of what was to come. After a minute, I opened my eyes, put on my helmet, and started the bike. As I crossed the Crazy Woman at the beginning of my third ride around the globe, I was almost more anxious to return than to get into the flow of another long ride, hoping that when I did return I would have answers to haunting questions. Close to the top of the list was what many would think crazy—how to catch a fish. In the meantime, I had a lot of the world to ride, and the Crazy Woman would see me cross her again.

Sellers offer goods in the floating market near Bangkok where I stopped for a few items.

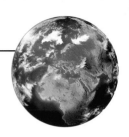

THE RIDE
OF A LIFETIME

One day in October 1912, American advertising writer Carl Stearns Clancy and his riding partner, Walter Storey, set out on the first known motorcycle ride around the globe. We know Clancy and Storey used Henderson motorcycles and paid part of their expenses by writing articles for magazines and newspapers along the way. We even know part of their route, as outlined by Clancy in an article that appeared in the March 4, 1913, issue of *The Bicycling World and Motorcycle Review*:

> *Our route as laid out now covers fourteen European, one African and four Asiatic countries, besides including the Philippines, Hawaii and a new transcontinental route back from the Pacific. Our mileage in Europe will be about 5,500, in Africa 400, in Asia 5,000, in the United States and dependencies 3,500—a total of 14,000 on land miles besides 15,000 on water—all to be covered in one year.*

Clancy finished the ride but Storey did not, being "imperatively called back to America," according to his partner. Nearly a century later, many riders have followed Clancy's example and circled the globe on their motorcycles. I have made the journey four times myself. For all of us, traveling around the world by motorcycle has been the ride of a lifetime.

Why Ride
Around the World?

People take to globe-trotting on a motorcycle for many reasons. Clancy and Storey felt "supersaturated by work" and wanted "to invest a year's time in something else than the everlasting chase for the dollar." Other riders run from unhappy relationships or jobs, from lifestyles no longer desired. One famed motorcycle traveler chose to abandon parenthood, opting for ten years on the road over ten years of supporting a family. Another chose to leave the massage parlors of her native Slovenia in hopes of chang-

ing her career from masseuse to photographer or journalist. For others, the promise of an extended ride around the globe is the carrot to get them through a long and difficult task. American Dave Barr, who lost both legs to a land mine while in Angola, dangled that carrot from the end of a rehabilitation stick. His dream was to get out of the hospital bed and back on to his Harley-Davidson, and then ride that bike around the world. Eventually, he did.

Some riders want to see the world—but not from the inside of a car, bus, train, or airplane. They want to be part of the environment they are passing through, part of the changing world around them. Others are merely looking for a long vacation, and they want to take it on a motorcycle as a way to enjoy life on the road. One couple I met had taken a global ride for

The call of being on the road has four times pulled me around the globe. Sometimes I make a record of where I have been to share, other times I have been selfish and kept the memories and images to myself.

On a road in Wyoming, Nick Sanders takes a rare break during his record-shattering thirty-one-day world ride in 1997. It was startling to meet a British motorcyclist in the middle of nowhere, USA, with little luggage and time, racing around the globe.

their honeymoon. Then there are the true explorers, those adventure seekers who 150 years ago would have been riding horses into unknown territory, whether the blistering sands of the Sahara Desert or the humid, mosquito-infested rainforest of the Amazon.

One of my British friends, Nick Sanders, set out to ride around the world solely for the purpose of securing a spot in the book of *Guinness World Records*. He had been around the world three times previously, twice by bicycle and once by motorcycle. His goal this time was to become the fastest man around the globe on a motorcycle. The route he chose can best be described as the one with the longest, straightest, fastest roads. He achieved his goal in thirty-one days and twenty hours. A rider named Mariola Cichon wanted to become the first American woman to ride solo around the globe, thereby setting a record for U.S. women motorcyclists. Unfortunately, she wrecked in Gambia, and severe injuries brought her journey to a halt. While she hopes to eventually continue her ride, the totaled motorcycle and long road to physical and financial recovery may make that impossible.

Global riders have told me they left to seek answers to questions about everything from why they could not find love to whether they should pursue an alternative religion or lifestyle. Some found answers, others returned home with the same questions—not particularly wiser but certainly older.

Others are those who make the ride to become recognized, to become important. They use it as a base to promote themselves as a business, using their fame to sell books or DVDs or launch a career as a tour guide or start a

TRAVELING MY WAY

When I travel around the world, I often hear other motorcyclists say, "When I retire, I want to do what you do—go see different places on my motorcycle." I smile, wish them the best, and offer to help if I can. But deep down I know they will never do it. When they retire they will be too old to do what I do. Even now I am starting to suffer the creaks and cracks of my bones I used to ignore. When I ride into a town past a motel, I find myself wishing to use its fresh sheets, bed, TV, air-conditioning, telephone, hot shower, toilet, and locks that work.

At best, upon retirement my wishful friends will sign up for a guided two-week motorcycle tour that costs more than I spend in six months of travel. I am not saying that's bad. It's good they will live their dreams within their limits. I do know they will not want to travel like I do, sleeping in a tent on the ground behind some gas station in Argentina while trucks roll in and out all night, because I have to manage Argentina on $1,000 for the month. Wanting to do what I do, how I do it, is not really their dreams.

Australians Ken and Carol Duval load up their BMW for the next stage of their global journey. They rode two-up, carrying everything they needed, often camping at night to make their budget go as far as it could.

touring business. For them a ride 'round the world is part of a business plan.

Then there are the two-wheel dreamers, a number of them not even motorcyclist enthusiasts, whose imaginations have been captured by books written by world travelers. These readers have become so enamored with the journey an author has depicted that they, too, set out to circle the globe. Some wish to describe themselves and the world they pass through by writing their own books or articles about their travels. My imagination was first captured by American motorcyclist Danny Liska's book *Two Wheels to Adventure*, which contains hundreds of black-and-white photos and tales of his North and South American adventures. As far as I'm concerned, it still ranks as the best motorcycle adventure book ever published.

Liska rode his two BMWs to the ends of the earth in the 1960s. I remember seeing posters of him somewhere deep in the South American jungles in my local BMW motorcycle shop and saying to myself, "Hmm, a guy can really ride to South America?" Those posters, plus some magazine articles about Liska, sold me on my first BMW, a 1969 R69US. Though I only used my bike to beat my Triumph-riding friends around curves, I never lost my memories of Liska and his BMW. From his pictures, I could see that he rode his motorcycle through the toughest places on earth, and it hooked me on long-distance travel.

Another well-known globe-trotting author is Ted Simon, who wrote *Jupiter's Travels*. At the time I began reading the book, I was commuting daily from home to school and to work on a motorcycle. On weekends, I was

I discovered this small and quietly beautiful road while riding through Austria. Often I will purposely "forget" the exact location of a road so I can experience the surprise and pleasure of finding it again.

racing the same bike on paved road racing tracks up and down the East Coast. However, I put the book down after reading only a couple of chapters. The picture Simon was painting of riding an unreliable Triumph around the world made about as much sense to me then as hiking across the Gobi Desert with no tent, sleeping bag, water, or food. Even if it was an adventure, it seemed a doomed one. Much later, near the end of the 1980s, after I had met Simon and made one long ride around the world myself, I picked up the book again. I was curious to know how his ride compared with mine and if he had seen the world as I had seen it.

My 'Round-the-World Travels

The first of my four 'round-the-world trips was unplanned and stretched from the 1960s into the 1980s. During that time, one of the themes of my motorcycling life was to hunt out good roads. In 1970, I flew to Europe, purchased a new BMW R75/5, and hunted for roads in the Alps and the Pyrenees. Riding through countries where I did not know the language and crossing borders taught me that neither language nor borders were major barriers to riding outside of the United States. Rides into Canada and Mexico had showed me that getting me and a motorcycle out of the United States was relatively simple.

In the late 1980s, I found enough time and money to chase rumors of other good motorcycling roads around the globe. I managed to bag what I had been told were superb roads in North and Central America, Europe, Australia, and New Zealand. Along the way, my route took me into parts of Africa and Asia (more to sightsee than to notch up roads).

One night after returning to the United States from the latest excursions, I was tracing my route on a globe with a traveling friend when he said, "You know, while you were out there, you actually rode completely around the world." That surprised me because making a world trip had not been my goal. As a motorcyclist who enjoys riding good roads—fast—I had been seeking out the best roads on the planet, not following a circumscribed route. That's why I call that first trip around the world my I Got Lost Ride. Someone looking at the route I followed and the time it took to finish the journey could only conclude that I had gotten lost, especially given the numerous times I backtracked to take a second ride on an exceptionally good road.

My second ride around the world came about as the result of meeting Bernd Tesch, a German travel book "aficionado." He was of the opinion that a valid ride around the world had

A huge hand rises from the Atacama Desert on the Pan American Highway in Chile. The painted graffiti on the cement hand reminded me of "alley art" in the States.

to be preplanned, with the stated purpose of the ride being to circle the globe on a motorcycle. I disagreed, arguing that unless riders wanted an outsider's validation—which I felt was unnecessary and worthless—they did not need to file "flight plans" with Tesch or anyone else and then follow them. Whether a motorcyclist had a plan or not, if he or she eventually crossed all twenty-four time zones, rode to a point on the other side of the

globe from the starting place, and began and finished at the same location, then that motorcyclist had indeed circled the globe.

Tesch's insistence on the "flight plan" scenario seemed based more on his desire to write a book about world rides—and thus his hope of securing as much ready information as he could from those who would tell him of their routes and dates—than anything else. Although I didn't agree with him, I contacted the people at Guinness World Records for their opinion. They, too, said that I needed a plan and sent me their guidelines. However, those guidelines were loose, not strict rules, and they were only applicable if the a morotcyclist wanted to be granted a Guinness Record.

While I was not interested in a Guinness World Record—knowing the records rewarded such feats as shoving the most nails up your nose and eating the most worms—I did decide to make a long ride around the world following some of the guidelines. However, those guidelines were loose, not strict rules, and they were only applicable if the motorcyclist wanted to be granted a Guinness Record.

On my second world trip, begun in 1997, I set out with the plan of riding my motorcycle to the points farthest north and south on the globe that could be reached by road: Prudhoe Bay, Alaska; Ushuaia, Argentina; Cape Agulhaus, South Africa; and the North Cape, Norway. While I was at it, I took a side trip to Bluff, New Zealand. I called this my Ride to the Ends of the Earth. By the time it was over in 2000, I had reached my touch points, crossed the equator four times, worn out a

My overloaded motorcycle rests on its cylinder, not a side stand, on this little path in New Zealand. The woman I was shepherding "down under" during my third circumnavigation did not like off-pavement riding, so I would explore the more difficult tracks alone.

couple of motorcycles, and burned through a large stack of money.

About halfway through my second journey, I met a woman who was trying to set a Guinness World Record for riding solo around the world and touching all seven continents. I was going the opposite direction, at a much faster pace, but we bonded so I agreed to help her with her pursuit. She was a novice, never having ridden a motorcycle before beginning her journey. Tesch had advised her to contact me while in the United States, her first long leg, but I had been in South America at the time. Our paths crossed as I was leaving South America and she was entering Caracas, Venezuela. She had shipped her BMW F650 out of Florida, but the shipping company had lost it between Florida and Venezuela, stranding her in Caracas. She had been there a month before we met, e-mail-

ing, writing, and calling the freight forwarder in Florida, trying to locate her motorcycle. I spent a few hours helping her with her hunt as I was preparing to ship out my bike. I eventually located the large crate with her BMW—sitting in the Caracas airport customs department, where it had been for some time.

Six months later, she was still moving at a snail's pace through South America. Not long after, her travel plan fell apart when she discovered how much it would cost to send her bike from Ushuaia, Argentina, to Antarctica on a Canadian ship. Fortunately, having explored this option myself, I knew the shipping from Ushuaia could be done more cheaply by dealing directly with the captain of the cruise ship. She followed my advice, saved herself $2,500, and managed to ride about 50 meters on the seventh continent, all she needed for that leg of her Guinness World Record.

She then asked me to join her in New Zealand, where she would have to learn to ride on the left side of the road. I had liked New Zealand on previous rides and thought there might be a book idea in the trip so I agreed. I stopped my deskwork in the United States, flew to New Zealand, borrowed a motorcycle, and spent a month guiding her on the North and South Islands.

While I was riding in New Zealand, an idea struck me: Why waste money shipping a motorcycle across bodies of water just so I could maneuver myself around the world on the same bike? Why not try something different? I could make a global ride by changing motorcycles at each crossing and carrying my gear with me, much as the Pony Express riders had changed horses on their mail runs between Missouri and California. To make the trip interesting, I would use only motorcycles manufactured on the continent I was riding across. As I began planning, I realized I could never find a motorcycle manufactured in Antarctica, Africa, or Australia, so I crossed those continents off my list. For the remaining four continents, I ended up using a 1947 Indian and a Harley-Davidson in North America; a BMW in Europe; Enfield, SYM, Honda, and Hartford motorcycles in Asia; and an Amazonas for South America. This variety of motorcycles had handshifters, foot clutches, and rear brakes on the left side and foot shifters on the right—and one had no shifter at all.

I began my third journey around the world in fall 2001. About this time, my Guinness World Record–chasing friend was worrying about crossing India because she had heard that riding motorcycles in India and Nepal could

Friend and fellow circumnavigator Sharon Whitman poses with the Harley-Davidson she chose for her ride of a lifetime.

be very dangerous. She asked if I would guide her through India (and eventually Nepal and Bangladesh). I told her I would, working those places into my own goal.

Arriving in Delhi, India, with my helmet and riding equipment, I purchased a new Enfield 500cc Bullet, then headed to Nepal to meet my Guinness traveler. It took me a month to dislodge her from Katmandu, probably because of her fear of riding in India. Eventually, though, her visa expired and we left. The Indian state of Sikkim (located in the Himalayas), Bangladesh, and Nepal were challenging to get through. This was due not so much from difficulties involving riding skills as to a lack of observed road rules and etiquette and from obstacles ranging from potholes to farmers drying wheat on the road to animals and people aimlessly wandering. Everything in this region moved at a fairly slow pace. My first day on the road out of Delhi was an indication of the challenge ahead: I was hit four times, none hard, but enough for me to start wondering if the traffic in Rio de Janeiro, Mexico City, Cairo, and Tokyo had really been as bad as I remembered.

Riding in India was probably the worst highway riding I have experienced in the world. The roads were in poor condition, the vehicles were often worse, and drivers seemed to heed no rules. Survival was based on a hierarchy of the bigger vehicle's having the right of way, and yet even this rule was ignored. Minivans filled with people would collide head-on with semitrucks, neither driver willing to give way while each was passing a slower vehicle. Buses would plow through crowds of people, cars would crash into slower moving tractors, and bicycle riders would be

A camel train ambles down a road in India while my motorcycle sits idle on the other side. In that country, I wisely yielded to the "other guy," especially when they were bigger (camels, elephants) or more sacred (cows).

My learning curve on aluminum panniers began in the early 1970s, while I was riding through Europe. I quit using the manufacturers' plastic saddlebags after losing an expensive Bavarian set, which not only failed to keep my gear dry but also cracked at the hinges. By this time, I knew my style of riding exceeded the manufacturers' expectations for what their optional saddlebags would endure.

At one point, I had fitted some French leather saddlebags to my BMW, but they leaked. Earlier, I had tried a high-end English fiberglass set of boxes, which not only leaked but also cracked the first time the motorcycle flopped over—an expensive loss. In an Italian campground, I met a Swiss traveler who had made a pair of aluminum top-opening boxes two millimeters thick, which were ugly but kept everything inside dry. He assured me they would not crumple or crack if the bike tipped over and were maintenance free.

Back in the States, I hunted for something like the Swiss set, finally settling on a pair of army-surplus steel ammunition boxes, each heavier than a cinderblock but nearly indestructible and completely waterproof. They carried more gear than the plastic and leather motorcycle saddlebags I had previously tried and cost just five dollars for the pair (versus several hundred dollars for the factory offerings). On a trip to Alaska, however, I found that the motorcycle's subframe could not carry the weight of the heavy boxes and all the gear inside. It cracked. I had to design a carrying system that would support the weight of the boxes and tie it into the main frame, which took the weight off the subframe. I also found a smaller set of ammo boxes.

During a trip to Europe in the early 1980s, I discovered some German alu-

These homemade aluminum panniers and top box by Grant Johnson saw twelve years around the world.

minum boxes, Darr Adventure Boxes. Unfortunately, when attached they made my motorcycle about five feet wide across the back. However, I soon found a way to compensate for the upswept muffler and pulled them closer to the seat.

On subsequent trips to Europe, I started to notice different models of boxes, some with specially designed mounting frames and luggage racks. I brought the more promising versions back to use on my various motorcycles. On one trip, a German distributor approached me about importing his brand. I agreed, but that effort failed when he could not deliver on a timely basis. Soon, other importers were bringing in their brands, and a few small American firms started making their own.

The demand was there—enduro and dual-sport riders wanted boxes that were durable, functional, and reasonably priced. The increasing niche market of adventure riders created even more demand. Today, there are at least a dozen American suppliers of aluminum panniers and racks, some major manufacturers, such as BMW and KTM, also offer aluminum panniers or boxes as accessories.

A cow helps herself to the grain on the back of an overloaded truck in India. The Indians nearby made nothing of the impromptu bovine meal, but they did find the sight of a motorcycle set up for touring very curious.

mowed down by anything bigger and faster. It was not unusual to find a car or truck riding down the wrong side of the road, expecting everything in its path to give way. Motorcycles rode near the bottom of the hierarchy, and thus many times were run off the road and onto the footpath running parallel to the pavement.

About the only thing safe on a road in India is a cow because of its sacredness—or an elephant because of its sheer size. To avoid hitting a cow in the road, a car or truck will swerve into oncoming traffic, perhaps killing numerous people. I could not ride a single day without coming upon a fatal accident. I have likened traffic on Indian roads to what one could expect watching the activity of ants on an anthill if you poured gas on it and lit it. The carnage and blood on the roads of

India exceeds any I have seen elsewhere in the world. In other countries, "roadkill" is usually a reference to dead animals; in India it is more likely a reference to human victims.

Once I got Ms. Record Chaser and myself across India, I sold the Enfield and started focusing on Taiwan, which has the world's highest accident rate for motorcyclists. Once in Taiwan, I discovered the high accident rate was mostly due to the great number of little motorcycles—millions of them! The drivers were not bad (compared with those in India), but there were just so many. After two weeks there, I boarded a flight to Los Angeles and spent some final days on a Harley-Davidson Ultra Classic on the last leg home to Montana. During my trip, I had crossed the equator twice, driven through four continents, and seen parts of the world through the eyes of a female newbie. It had been a long, strange ride.

After my third global ride, editors at *Motorcycle Con-sumer News* posed an interesting question to me, "What would you do to make a motorcycle you are unfamiliar with ready for a ride around the world?" Six months later, I had the answer on its center stand in my studio. With a lot of help from others, I had prepared a Kawasaki for a global ride. Along the way, I had recorded the work in photos, written articles about the modifications, and taken test rides. The Kawasaki, I concluded, was ready to make a global trip. With the experience and knowledge gained from three previous rides around the world, I was ready to stamp my approval on the motorcycle—almost.

The Kawasaki looked right, but a 0.03 percent sliver of doubt nagged at me, doubt about some of the choices I had made for modifications. Would the engine survive the heat of the Sahara Desert, since I had lowered the gearing, changed the coolant, and modified the flow of air past the radiator? I had bolted on aftermarket items such as aluminum panniers, engine guards, tank panniers, a windscreen, and mirrors—would something work loose? Had I picked the right tires, the right inner tubes? Did I have the right tools in the expanded kit?

As I walked around the Kawasaki, peering at modified frame bolts, the rear master cylinder brake, water pump guards, and clipped wires from the side stand that allowed the starter to work when the stand was down, my doubt disappeared. This bike was right. I shut off the lights in my studio and fell into bed, my last conscious thought, "Am I sure I did everything right?" Four months later, in March of 2002, I embarked on my fourth ride around the world on the Kawasaki.

Taiwanese motorcyclists rev their engines, ready to scream off the second the light turns green. At every stoplight in Taiwan, motorcycles move to the front and take off like it's the beginning of a Grand Prix race.

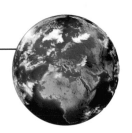

CHOOSING YOUR MOTORCYCLE

ithout a doubt, the one question I am asked the most is, "Which is the best motorcycle to take on a ride around the world?" My answer is always the same, "Whichever bike suits you." Your bike is your traveling partner, so you should use the one you prefer. I have seen everything from a 50cc Vespa to a heavyweight Harley-Davidson being piloted around the globe. All owners claim their bikes are the best. A BMW owner who tries to convince a Harley-Davidson lover that a BMW is a better bike to ride around the world will face a formidable task.

Argentinian Emilio Scotto rode his 1980 Honda Gold Wing twice around the world, tagging six continents, logging 485,000 miles, and touching 232 countries. After ten years, two months, and nineteen days with the Gold Wing, Scotto was unlikely to be convinced that there would have been a better motorcycle for his trip. Englishman Robbie Marshall chose to ride a Triumph around the world. Simon Milward built his own motorcycle using a 600cc Rotax engine (and parts purchased from a total of eight different countries), then setting off to circle the globe. In India, I met a Japanese rider whose choice was a 50cc Yamaha. He came to his decision based on fuel efficiency, the cost of the bike ($800 used), and the fact that the Yamaha had a driveshaft. What made his choice especially interesting was that he knew what he wanted before setting eyes on it. The Japanese postal system used this model for letter and package delivery, so in his mind the motorcycle, though well broken in before he started, was indestructible.

My favorite choices for long rides have included the BMW and Honda Gold Wing. Each has its advantages and disadvantages. The Gold Wing hates anything other than smooth, straight pavement, while the BMW manages gravel and dirt well. The BMW likes to break down; the Gold Wing likes to fall down. On my fourth ride around the world, I used the Kawasaki KLR 650cc I had modified. Other than requiring routine maintenance, such as oil and tire changes, the motorcycle performed flawlessly. I did not tighten a single spoke, replace a fuse, or once touch the carburetor. Clearly, it was not a bad choice, especially given the fact that I would have spent nearly 50 percent more for the same size BMW.

In choosing your world-ride motorcycle, you should consider several factors. Among them are cost and size, comfort, and durability, reliability, and simplicity. Sadly, some riders consider image to be an important factor, one outweighing many of the practical considerations.

Cost and Size

The first two factors for consideration, cost and size, are closely

This bits-of-this-bits-of-that bike on a street in Thailand has a two-stroke "tuk-tuk" engine and a reverse chain drive. It might seem like the perfect "world tourer" to someone with tons of luggage, but what would it be like when on a curve?

related. For instance, what you pay for a motorcycle depends not only on the make and model but on the size as well. Size also affects how much you have to pay in shipping costs. More importantly, you should realize that getting the biggest and the costliest motorcycle does not necessarily mean you are getting the best bike for you.

Cost

Motorcycle prices cover a broad range. For example, you might spend as little as $500 for a used Honda or as much as $25,000 for a fully equipped one. Therefore, the question of how much to spend on a bike may be determined in large part by how deep the traveler's pockets are. My number one rule for selecting a motorcycle for global travel: never take one you cannot afford to lose. With the quality of motorcycles manufactured today, a new $5,000 model can make a ride around the world as easily as a fully equipped $30,000 one. If your bike is stolen or badly crashed, you'll miss the $5,000 motorcycle less than the one costing six times as much. And you'll still have $25,000 left to purchase another bike.

One year when I was riding through Guatemala, I met a man on a large BMW road bike who offered to sell it to me at a bargain-basement price. He and his riding companion had begun their trip through Central America on new motorcycles, his partner on a Harley-Davidson, he on the BMW. At a street corner in Guatemala City, a man in a business suit had pulled a huge handgun out of a briefcase, pointed it at the Harley rider, and said, "Get off the bike." The rider did as instructed. The man set down his

Julian Bowyers stands atop his homemade three-wheel cycle, his choice of conveyance for a trip around the world.

briefcase, got on the Harley, and roared away. When the Americans opened the abandoned briefcase in hopes of discovering some clues to their thief's identity, all they found was an empty Ray-Ban sunglasses case—an expensive tradeoff for the $20,000 motorcycle. The BMW owner decided that riding an expensive motorcycle there was too risky and he would rather have half its worth than none. I passed on the deal, knowing that losing it, even at half the price, would still mean losing twice what my own bike was worth.

I also know motorcyclists who have spent more money getting their crashed or broken motorcycles out of foreign countries than the machines were worth. For instance, one Honda rider who crashed and broke his leg in Honduras insisted on flying his bike back to the United States. Given what he spent in time and money on crating and shipping, he paid dearly for the wrecked Honda, which had only sentimental value; he should have left it in Honduras. Before beginning his world tour, a well-heeled American bragged about spending $15,000 on his BMW and adding another $15,000 in accessories. Less than a week into his journey he crashed and had to abandon his ride; of course, he shipped the expensive motorcycle home, which likely cost him more than his own flight back. Another motorcyclist crashed his BMW in Yugoslavia and, tragically, died. His family spent more on the return of the totaled BMW than on shipping the man's remains back home.

By contrast, when a car in the wrong lane crashed head-on into Mariola Cichon and her Kawasaki in Africa, she left the wadded bike there. The motorcycle was the least of her worries, the bike's cost being far less than the huge medical bills she was incurring for two severely broken legs.

Size

When determining the cost of a motorcycle, size is an important consideration because it affects not only the purchase price but also shipping charges. On any ride around the world, many of the miles are going to be across water, which means conveyance by air or by boat. Shipping companies often charge by space or weight, whichever they compute to be higher. Obviously, if the shipper decides to use weight, the heavier motorcycle will cost more to transport. (The price a friend paid to get his BMW from the United States to Europe was three times what I paid for my 650cc Kawasaki.) Add the cost of transporting the bike across the Indian Ocean, then the Pacific, and you're looking at

Sixty-nine-year-old Arthur Zawodny, from Poland, mounts his 1997 SR 500 Yamaha, ready to continue across Russia before heading to America. He also owned a Gold Wing but chose the smaller bike for the longer ride because it was "something I can handle."

When choosing a motorcycle, consider tire size. In most countries, an 18-inch rear tire can usually be found. If your bike has an odd tire size and you are in a country where there are no dealers, such as Russia or China, you may have to wait several weeks for a tire to be shipped in. This can be expensive—you might have to pay as much as 100 percent the cost in customs tax—and it may take several days to get the tire through customs.

Urals, such as this customized model, could be found everywhere in Russia, which meant a traveler crossing the country on one could always find a knowledgeable mechanic and spare parts.

enough money to purchase several new motorcycles—one on each continent!

I also generally rule out heavyweight motorcycles because I prefer a bike I can pick up by myself when it falls over. Not so for some of my globe-riding friends. One German woman I met, unable to physically pick up her bike, simply left the fallen BMW motorcycle on its side when it toppled during her ride through Africa. When I asked her how she had managed to continue her trip with her bike in such a state, she smiled and said, "I turned off the gas and waited until someone, usually a man, came along and helped me pick it up."

While 800 pounds of motorcycle may seem agile in curves and parking lots, it is like wrestling a greased hog in a muddy pigsty when it gets on grass, mud, ice, or snow—the latter two possible anytime of the year in places such as Alaska. While the lighter motorcycle may go down just as quickly, chances are a dab (a quick foot touch on the road) or a lighter front end may keep a bike upright more often.

Be aware that what begins as a lightweight motorcycle can quickly become a heavyweight one when you are preparing it for a long ride. My preference is for a motorcycle that starts in the 400- to 500-pound range because after I add accessories, spare parts, tools, clothes, cameras, and myself, the overall weight approaches 700 pounds. If I started with a 700-pound motorcycle, then added my basic requirements, I'd soon be looking at 1,000 pounds. That weight is fine as long as the motorcycle is upright, on dry pavement, and moving in a straight line down Interstate 90 on a clear day. In other circumstances, stopping that half-tonner is another story.

Comfort

Comfort ranks high on the list when you're riding around the globe, logging anywhere from 20,000 to 60,000 miles. For example, many dual-sport motorcycles, while they are fine for a few hours of weekend riding, become machines of torture on any ride longer than half a day. The wind-

Who says you need a big bike for a big ride? This Japanese motorcyclist was trekking the globe on a 50cc.

screens do little to divert wind, the seats are nothing more than boards covered in vinyl, and the suspension systems, good for rocks and ruts, are stiff enough to clatter teeth on an interstate. At the other end of the spectrum you find the highway recliners, those heavy-weight motorcycles made for knocking down 1,000-mile days on interstates as smoothly as if you were riding inside a plastic bubble. Their heated seats can feel like magic fingers, and the plastic up front acts more like an automobile windshield than a windscreen. Add to that heated handgrips, CD players, and cup holders, and you might as well be sitting in your recliner, flipping through channels on your TV, as roaming on a motorcycle. My choice falls somewhere between these extremes. I like a bike that is reasonably comfortable to sit on

for six to eight hours per day, diverts the wind over my helmet and around my upper body, and vibrates less than a washing machine with a bowling ball inside.

For global rides, though, it's not just the model and make of a machine that matter. Where everything on the bike is located is important, too. One of my early mistakes was assuming that a motorcycle I found comfortable over a two-week vacation would suit me over a two-year journey. I discovered that little things, such as mirror location, foot peg height, lever angle, and handgrip size, mattered significantly on long rides. I could accept their slightly uncomfort-able locations on the short rides but grew to hate them on the long ones.

When I first started racing motor-cycles, I would spend hours in the shop

In Cuba, where bike accessories and shops are difficult to find (as in many developing countries), the owner of this bike solved his hard seat problem with a burlap sack.

of my mentor and adopted father, Stan Myers, sitting on my race bike without the motor running. He would have me place my hands, arms, legs, head, and backside in various positions, and then we would move around parts of the motorcycle to accommodate those positions, trying to find the right combination, the one most comfortable and aerodynamic. It wasn't easy. When my hands felt right, my elbows would stick out widely, acting as flaps that might slow me down in the wind. When we would get my arms tucked in tightly to my chest, my knees would be too high or the seat back too far forward. After hours of experimenting, we would start again.

A novice racer at the time, I saw these body placement experiments as foolish. What I wanted was speed, and

I thought we should be spending our time working on the engine in search of more horsepower. With the patience of Job, Stan would tell me time and again, "You need to be comfortable when going fast. Discomfort means distraction, and distraction can kill you."

He was right! I can still remember losing a race because my right hand cramped from muscle spasms. I could not get it to open, which meant I could not use the front brake, 75 percent or more of a bike's braking power. What had felt comfortable in the shop, when I had been sitting on the motorcycle for only a few minutes, became a disabling pain during a full-on 35-mile race. Now I apply some of those same theories to my 'round-the-world motorcycles. I practice positioning myself, moving foot pegs and seat, adjusting handlebar and lever angles, repositioning mirrors, windscreen, and tank panniers, until I become comfortable. I have also switched gas tanks for better knee positioning.

I am always in search of the perfect seat. A good seat is the most important factor in determining a rider's comfort. I do not know why motorcycle manufacturers cannot design a comfortable stock seat; that they cannot is proven by the millions of dollars spent each year on aftermarket seats. Fortunes have been made by companies smart enough to figure out how to comfortably accommodate men's and women's buttocks on bikes. Somewhere among all the mountains of junk found in the great Motorcycle Hell of Worthless Parts, you will find a mountain that towers over all the rest—composed of discarded motorcycle seats.

If you are going to ride around the world, the best seat is the one you can comfortably sit on—not for hours at a time, nor for days at a time, but for months at a time. It is one thing to plant your back end on a seat for ten days and quite another to rest it there for a long-distance trip logging up to 1,000 miles per day. A comfortable seat can be expensive, yet the most expensive seat is not always the best. For one of my long-ride motorcycles, I purchased a high-end, well-known, custom-built seat. It was a great improvement over the stock seat, but the more time I spent on the custom seat, the less comfortable it became. What started out as soft supple leather became tougher than the sole of a jump boot. Then the foam on the inside started to break down—and not evenly. Eventually, my left buttock was resting on a mounting bolt while the right was an inch higher.

The best seat I have ever used is one I modified to fit my original seat base

My overloaded bike sits in the deep sand, needing some work before I can get back on the road. Fortunately, I had food, water, some vodka, camping equipment, and a loose schedule, so I settled in for the night.

as well as my butt. I ordered an after-market seat for a Gold Wing from the JC Whitney mail order company. I ripped the old cover and foam off my original seat base, then went to work with a sharp knife and scissors to whittle down the Wing seat to fit my BMW motorcycle's smaller base. When I finished, I stapled the vinyl to the base and went for a long ride. After three days, I pulled the staples out, whittled some more, and tried the seat again. When I found what was comfortable, I glued the foam to the base and stapled the vinyl on for good. Thirty thousand miles later, I was still using that seat, never once having been uncomfortable. My cost was one-fifth what I had paid for the earlier custom seat.

Putting Taiwan's Hartford motorcycle to the test, I ride it up a rocky path on a hill military tanks used for practice maneuvers.

Durability, Reliability, and Simplicity

Three more important, and interrelated, factors are durability, reliability, and simplicity. If you don't have all three going for you, you may not be able to finish that world ride.

Durability

One marque (model of motorcycle) long known as a tough world tourer also has a reputation for breaking transmissions, chewing up driveshafts, and killing electrical systems. While the frame, engine, and wheels are among the toughest in the industry, these other parts fail the durability test.

Next to that infamous mountain of discarded motorcycle seats must be a pile almost as high of blown shock absorbers. Manufacturers' originals, they were designed for highway use but failed when pushed beyond the limit of anything harder than pavement riding with a light load. Durability needs to be qualified with respect to planned route, riding style, and carrying capacity.

For example, if you are going to stick to paved roads, ride solo (for a lighter load), and maintain a moderate pace, there is little need to spend $1,000 on shock absorbers or gusseting the frame. However, if you are planning on a run to Prudhoe Bay, some deep sand work across the Sahara, or a slog over jungle tracks in Brazil, then you should take a motorcycle made for the tough stuff.

For off-road riding, you should consider a model that has higher ground clearance and stronger suspension, one that falls into the "dual-purpose" or "adventure" category. Generally, these models come with standard modifications for off-pavement work. However, there are some drawbacks to these more aggressive models.

Because I was doing no off-pavement riding through Japan, this BMW R1100 RT was perfect for touring the country.

First, the word adventure is probably one of the most abused in motorcycling. A bike marketed as an adventure model may require expensive modifications before it is really ready to be taken for serious off-road riding, including aftermarket shocks, more aggressive tires, and fall-down protection such as crash bars. Usually these models fall into a category with SUVs—that is, better suited for posing than for handling the tough stuff. For some of these marketed "adventure tourers," the adventure is the adrenaline rush the buyer feels when presented with the final price tag.

Second, the more aggressive models tend to be less comfortable on the highways due to their reduction in weather protection and attempts to lower

weight. By the time buyers have added carrying capacity, weather protectors, softer seats, and larger gas tanks, they can be looking at a two-wheel SUV.

Third, the dual-sport models tend to be higher for better ground clearance, making them too tall for a vertically challenged rider. Although modifications in the form of custom seats and lowering kits can make the motorcycle manageable, they can, again, be expensive.

What you are looking for is a trade-off between something designed to be ridden off-pavement and take the knocks when it falls and something that is comfortable enough for long days of riding.

Reliability

Next to that pile of shock absorbers is a mound of failed starters, alternators, batteries, driveshafts, and rear drives that have stranded world travelers at the ends of the earth. When considering what motorcycle to use, you need to look into whether it is reliable on a global ride. Find out what problems certain bikes have regularly experienced. For instance, the Kawasaki KLR, a model used by many world riders, is susceptible to a spring failure in the engine. Though small and inexpensive to replace (less than five dollars), this part can eventually cause the motor to "grenade," killing an otherwise reliable engine. Today, it's a simple matter to replace the spring, but for years riders could only cross their fingers and hope it didn't break.

Forced repairs on the road can be incredibly expensive. A Swiss couple, traveling across the United States on a motorcycle marketed as an adventure tourer, found themselves with a $1,500 bill to repair a broken drive-

RIDING THE INTERNET

With the Internet speeding into daily life, more motorcyclists have made the choice to live on the road. Prior to the Internet, information about travel in foreign countries was often limited and outdated. Whereas in 1990 it could take weeks to learn the entry requirements for a solo motorcyclist to ride into Russia, today this information is only a click away—you can simply read other motorcyclists' Web sites about their Russian rides.

The Internet can also be a rider's lifeline. Vladimir Yarets, a 63-year-old deaf rider from Belarus, had his world ride saved by the Internet after a serious crash near Bloomington, Illinois, on October 13, 2003, left him with fractured hip, pelvis, arm, and legs, as well as a dead 350cc Jawa motorcycle. Word went out over the Internet, and help was on its way. Volunteers created a Web site for Yarets, and Russian-speaking volunteers visited Yarets and helped him communicate. In mid-2004, after nearly two months in a hospital

and several more months recovering, Yarets was back on the road riding a donated BMW F650GS and headed to South America. The Internet had made it, even a blind person, possible for him to continue living his dream.

With the Internet, riders can plan and book their trips, confirm hotel and airline reservations, and check border crossing information. The well-heeled Internet rider can even book a world tour complete with guides, chase trucks, GPS readings, and paperwork facilitators. The Internet has made it so easy to travel around the world by motorcycle that today it seems like almost anyone can do it.

Yet while the Internet is a wonderful tool for travelers, using it extensively can take much of the adventure out of a global ride. To me, true adventure includes risk. The Internet has made it possible to remove much of the risk of a world ride; for many people, the biggest challenge becomes finding an ATM machine.

Canadians Grant and Susan Johnson, seen here with their R80 GS, have created an Internet global motorcycle travelers network through their site www.horizonsunlimited.com, a wonderful aid for 'round-the-world riders.

shaft. This included having to rent a truck to haul the motorcycle out of the Utah desert and into the nearest motorcycle shop that could replace the driveshaft and pay for the labor to install it. Not included was the time the two of them lost from their vacation schedule.

A Belgian couple found themselves and their BMW in Ushuaia, Argentina—about as far from a BMW motorcycle shop as they could ride—with a dead starter. The nearest dealer quoted them a price of $1,600 (about four times the Belgian cost) to have a replacement shipped in. This included not only the starter but also import taxes and shipping. The couple decided on an alternate plan. They waited for several weeks in Ushuaia while family members bought the part in Belgium, removed the receipt, wrapped the package in Christmas gift paper, and sent it by airmail as a present—all for less than $500.

So what is the best way to find reliability? The first trick is not to believe any advertising. Pictures of a male model sitting on a motorcycle in Africa are images advertising agencies are paid to create—all in the name of selling you the product. The best information on what is reliable comes from those who have used the product. With the Internet, it is easy to join a list or group that specializes in the motorcycle you are thinking of taking on your journey. After that, don't be afraid to use these four words: I need your help.

Simplicity

No matter how durable and reliable a motorcycle is in general, parts can still

This Belgian couple has settled into a campground in Ushuaia, Argentina, for three weeks while waiting for expensive BMW parts to arrive from Belgium. They got to know everyone in town, including the dogs.

fail, forcing you to make repairs. That's why I prefer keeping the equipment on my motorcycle simple. My most modern long rider, the Kawasaki KLR, was about as simple a bike as could be found on the market. Simplicity, however, is becoming more difficult to achieve these days as manufacturers move from carburetors to fuel-injection systems, and computerized and electronic gizmos become so complicated that no one but their designers understand them. Ten years ago, you could carry almost any replacement part you would ever need in a shoebox. Today if your BMW F650GS burps and sputters, unless you have a laptop computer with the right software (and only BMW dealers can purchase the software), you must vector into the nearest BMW motorcycle dealership and let them plug your bike into their computer to make the necessary adjustments. While I did carry a few electronic black boxes on my Kawasaki, none were equal to the $1,500 spare electronic brain (a preprogrammed black box) my BMW friend had to carry for his R1100GS.

If you plan to take a fairly easy route around the world, staying near major and modern cities, then maintaining simplicity may not be an issue. Flying a mechanic, with his laptop and a box full of spare electronic components, into Chita, Russia, from Europe is definitely only for high-end riders. These upscale motorcyclists may also choose to carry everything they need, including a mechanic, in a truck that follows them on their rides.

Some manufacturers will argue that their equipment is so well constructed these days that nothing will go wrong. If you believe that, then buy what they

One of the simplest motorcycles still being manufactured on the planet is the Ural. I prefer more modern simplicity.

have to offer, go for the top of the line, and join an Internet group specific to your motorcycle. If the motorcycle dies on the road, at least you have a lot of people ready to help, interested in validating their purchases or just curious to see if you or anyone else can make the needed repairs. My Guinness World Record chaser discovered how expensive making repairs can be when it cost her more than $8,000 to repair her BMW F650 in Japan—more than the motorcycle cost new.

The simpler the motorcycle, the easier and more convenient it is to get these things done on your path around the world. Finding motorcycle shops with trained mechanics and necessary parts is a cost and time factor you need to plan into your trip. If you have plenty of time and money, by all means chance a ride across the eight time zones of Russia on your gizmo-techno bike. However, if you are like me, you will choose a motorcycle simple enough that you can keep it running until you reach a mechanical oasis. While I am not a certified mechanic, I can do basic repairs and maintenance work, such as changing oil, gas filters,

tires, and plugs; adjusting valves; and tightening chains. If you don't know how to do any of this type of work, I suggest taking one of the many courses that are offered on the subject before setting out.

Image

Then there is the image factor. A group of German riders spent thousands of dollars each on purchasing motorcycles, spare tires, parts, riding clothing, and gear; then they hired a truck and driver to accompany them across the Sahara, carrying gas, spares, tents, water, and food. After they reached the end of the track and stood around swilling cold beer and congratulating one another on their success, a lone British rider came out of the desert on their same track. He was on a Honda CX 500, had two Army surplus packs tied on the back, and wore a leather flight cap, goggles, and a pair of hiking boots. The Germans were aghast as he flogged up to them in the deep sand. They asked how far he had come, and he told them, "I followed your tracks."

They sneered and snickered, speaking in German, which they thought he could not understand. "He's lying, no way could he have been behind us. It took us a week. Where did he get gas? Water? Look at him. He's not dressed for it, and that Honda is junk." So they decided to submit him to a truth test. They asked in English, "How did you get gas? There are no stations out there!"

"When I ran out, I waited until a Rover or truck came along and borrowed from them. Someone always lent me some," he replied.

A family proud of their unique "touring machine" rides down a street in Cuba.

Then the Germans asked him, "OK, how about food and water?"

"They'd let me have that, too."

Finally, one exasperated German said, "You don't even have any spare parts. I don't believe you."

The Brit reached in his leather jacket and pulled out a spark plug. Holding it up, he said, "Yes, I did."

The Germans are probably still scoffing because the Brit and his motorcycle did not fit their images of a global bike and biker. I believe him. Spending $10,000 to $20,000 on as a bike seen as tough, reliable, and image-correct tourer is not for me. I can buy the same bike for half the price if I ignore the image factor; I'd rather have more money left for the ride itself.

My Choices

For my four trips around the world, I rode several different bikes. Two of my favorite long-ride motorcycles are the BMW GS and the Kawasaki KLR 650. The BMW is the original adventure tourer, long favored by 'round-the-world bikers. A later arrival on the global-biking scene, the Kawasaki is not only durable and reliable but also much less expensive than the BMW.

I was partial to the BMW GS models because they were simple, could be ridden off-pavement and, at the time, were inexpensive to purchase second-hand. I could buy a low mileage GS for $1,500 to $2,500, a good starting point. Having owned several, I had also learned their weaknesses and how to prevent failure and improve them. Sadly, the GS has become more of a "cult bike" as it has grown older.

Recently, one sold for $6,500—nearly $6,000 more than book value. On a bike that old, a rule of thumb for value is about $1.00 per cc, so that 800cc bike should be worth only $800.

The second most popular make of bike I had noticed making global loops over the years was the Yamaha XT, known in Europe as the "poor man's BMW." Again, it was a simple motorcycle, inexpensive, did well off-pavement, and had a good global network of dealers for parts and service. However, in the late 1990s it was discontinued and replaced as tough budget tourer by the Kawasaki KLR 650. This model had been around nearly fifteen years by then, so there were numerous aftermarket manufacturers for improved parts and accessories and, at $4,999, it was good value.

BMW G/S

During the 1960s and 1970s, the BMW was popularized as a sound mechanical motorcycle when adventurers pushed it farther into uncharted areas around the globe. In the early 1980s, the BMW 800cc R80 G/S model developed a reputation for dependability by winning the rugged Paris-to-Dakar races. Europeans were quick to equate the model's Paris-to-Dakar dependability with an aptitude for long-distance riding. What most people didn't realize at the time was that these race-winning motorcycles were about as close to stock BMWs as elephants are to cheetahs: they had been completely modified from the tires up by the HPN Company of Germany. Numerous adventurers further popularized the R80s by selling magazine stories of their travels. In 1985, American Ed

Culberson did flog a nearly stock R80 G/S through the famed Darien Gap, becoming the first man to ride the jungle track from Panama to Colombia.

BMW's savvy marketing folks capitalized on their bike's wins in the deserts of Africa and the glowing tales of global wanderers by touting the GS as the "adventure tourer" and inventing a new class of motorcycle at the same time. From 1980 to 1987, BMW produced 21,864 of the R80 G/S bikes. What no one was touting were the stories of the transmissions dying and rotors flying apart as riders unknowingly pushed these bikes beyond their practical applications. No one thought to ask how many modifications HPN had made to the Paris-to-Dakar models or how many transmissions mechanics changed at overnight pit stops. HPN had pitched the stock electrical systems so even the riders didn't know that rotors and diode boards died.

Because of its popularity, the cost of an R80 G/S was high for many years.

My world-touring R80 G/S now has nearly 200,000 miles on it.

When a new and upgraded 1000cc model replaced the R80 G/S in the United States in 1987, the price of the R80 G/S fell to a wholesale level below $1,000. If a buyer was patient, he could find a spotless R80 G/S for $1,000 to $1,500. In the meantime, prices for the new BMW GS models started to move upward, grabbing an increasingly higher-income consumer. Currently, with taxes, delivery, and set-up costs, the price of a BMW R1200GS "adventure tourer" can easily equal that of a well-equipped new car. This steady movement up the price scale for the BMW GS models, together with the continuing adventure stories of global wandering in the media, has created an unusual market demand for the older air-cooled GS models. One of thses bikes was recently advertised for more than $8,000.

I limited the acquisition price of my BMW to $3,000. The model was actually more expensive than that, but after selling off some of the unwanted accessories that came with the motorcycle, the final cost was $3,000. You can get a good R100GS for about that price but, again, some parts might have to be sold. My most recent R100GS purchase cost only $1,500, but the transmission was dead and unchangeable and it required a new rear shock. So by the time I had finished preparing the bike, my cost was still in the $3,000 range.

The Kawasaki KLR

For my fourth ride around the world, I rode a Kawasaki KLR 650, a fairly basic bike with a water-cooled, single-cylinder, four-stroke engine and a five-speed transmission. In my travels, I had noticed this motorcycle almost as much as I had noticed the BMWs. Kawasaki has been pumping out these affordable motorcycles since 1987, making very few changes, and over the years, it has earned an enviable reputation for durability and manageability both on- and off-road. Due to its longevity, there is a proliferation of aftermarket suppliers offering everything from improved electrical components and softer seats to center stands and luggage. The KLR has become the perfect budget global tourer.

MOTORCYCLE PREPARATION

Preparation of the motorcycle takes more time than the actual planning of the trip. A well-prepared motorcycle can carry the rider around the world without a burp or gurgle while a poorly prepared one can make a long trip feel like a ride through Hades.

I have prepared several motorcycles for global rides and watched others do the same. Some over-prepare, some do the opposite. One of my over-prepared friends took the time to safety-wire his spokes—an off-road practice used mostly by motocross riders—yet never left the pavement during his entire global ride. Another friend bought a second-hand BMW and did little more than strap on his tent and sleeping gear before heading off, then wondered why he became stranded in the jungles of Brazil with a dead motorcycle. After expensive repairs, the bike came briefly back to life, only to die again when the driveshaft failed.

Some motorcyclists have chosen to go with new bikes, others with used. One rider I know paid $15,000 for a new BMW, then added another $15,000 worth of changes and accessories. Another chose a used bike and rebuilt it from the ground up. Within my moderate price range, I have done both.

Alterations and Accessories

No matter which motorcycle you choose for your global ride, there are some accessories you should add and alterations you should consider making—in addition to getting rid of the uncomfortable stock seat! The most important of these concern carrying capacity, fuel reserves, electrical and suspension systems, and protection from the elements and crashes.

Carrying Capacity

Carrying capacity should be one of the first considerations when looking at the adventure tourer. As discussed, I get rid of the original equipment because I've found that while it is fine for the weekend warrior,, it fails with rugged, long-term use.

The first aftermarket purchase should be panniers for the back to

I saw the rock in this desert at the last moment, just in time to scrub off about 20 mph and yell loudly. Surprises in the form of rocks and King salmons are good reasons to give your bike added protection when preparing it for a long ride.

increase carrying capacity. I have tried the plastic ones (some modified camera-carrying boxes, others that look like tourist luggage), but in the end, I always return to aluminum. Aluminum panniers are the squared side boxes placed where leather saddlebags usually would hang. To an old-timer, they look like the containers that the milkman used to leave milk bottles on the front doorstep. To the adventuring aficionado, they are a strong statement that proclaims, "Beware! Adventure seeker on board!"

If you want to use an aluminum pannier yet keep things simple, use the basic box. It attaches to a flat mounting system, allows for easy packing, and is usually priced at the lower end of the scale. On the downside, the basic box tends to stick out farther to the sides. An upswept exhaust muffler frequently compounds the width problem. To offset the protruding box syndrome, a narrower box can be mounted on the muffler side. Yet while the overall width will be reduced, the motorcycle will appear to be unbalanced from the rear.

Another option is to purchase a system in which the panniers are cut to fit the rear section of the motorcycle. However, as one hardened traveler found, "more cuts mean more welds, which mean more places where the panniers can crack." While the molded system may be fine for the weekend warrior who seldom ventures off-pavement, the same system can fail numerous times for the globe rider who is trying to cross Africa.

If you can't decide what size to get, remember that the bigger the box, the more you can carry. At the same time,

My BMW is prepared for its trek around the globe. Ted Simon, seen inspecting it at right, later decided to use one outfitted similarly on his second journey around the world. I like to think my setup helped him make his ride a success.

big boxes can cause problems. For example, one traveler learned the hard way how his low-hanging pannier could jump up and bite him. He caught his heel under one while paddling through sand. His leg broke, and he spent more than six weeks recuperating in Africa. He finally jettisoned the boxes when he realized he did not need the camping and cooking gear he was carrying—he accepted the fact that he was a hotel guy and rarely camped or cooked during travels around the world.

You can also increase carrying capacity by adding a tank bag. I prefer the larger tank bag because completely filled (preferably with lightweight items such as clothing) it serves as a wind and water shield when the weather is cold or wet. (However, if filled they become cumbersome and unwieldy when riding off-road.) To avoid problems, buy a waterproof cover for your tank bag; these covers are available for several models. Finally, I like a tank bag with an easy loading clear plastic top for maps and some side pockets for easy access to items such as an air gauge, pens, small bottles of water, and food.

Don't forget to test the function of your tank bag once it is in place. To get to the gas cap under the tank bag, you might have to loosen the mounting straps or disconnect one set entirely. Some models slide off the tank completely. One system I found, with a secured base and zippered top, worked fine until the plastic zipper died. Then I had to unstrap the entire tank bag merely to get the zipper to work—talk about frustrating!

As a final consideration, take a look at the material on the bottom of the tank bag. Some tank bags are designed to be supple, so as not to scratch the paint, but this allows the bag to slip around even when securely fastened. I prefer a rubberlike material that "grabs" the paint, caring far less about scratches than about function.

Fuel Reserves

Although the gas tank on stock motorcycles can be adequate for short trips or traveling around most of North America, you may want to add an extra-large plastic tank depending on the areas through which you plan to travel. Why add a tank? First, you may be able to double your fuel capacity. Second, the optional tank carries the fuel lower than does the stock tank, thereby lowering the motorcycle's center of gravity. (This is particularly important if you venture off-road or you find yourself struggling with a fully loaded motorcycle.) In addition, the tank is constructed of nearly clear plastic, which allows you to see how much gas is remaining.

Another reason to add an aftermarket tank is that some of them come with two fuel petcocks, one on each side; versus the stock tank, which may have only a single petcock. With two petcocks—and thus, four open positions (two "ons" and two reserves)—I can have one "on" position and three

With this plastic aftermarket tank this rider can carry nearly 10 gallons of fuel. Gas station attendants are often surprised when motorcyclists fill up such tanks.

reserves as I go from on-left to on-right, then to reserve-left and finally to reserve-right. Lastly, an aftermarket plastic tank takes knocks from rocks a little better than does a motorcycle's original steel tank.

Electrical and Suspension Systems

Batteries can be a mystery. What looks new on the outside actually can be close to dead on the inside. Before I begin any long ride, I invest in a new battery. I also recommend replacing all the lights, including those in the dash indicator. Replacement is cheap enough insurance against potential problems later on, and you can utilize the old lights as spare parts.

You might have to make modifications to the electrical system as well. For example, on the R80 G/S and well into the production of the R100GS, there are a number of electrical gremlins that need attending to prior to setting off on any ride that will take you far away from the local BMW electrical supply depot. The book *Classic Boxer Charging* by Rick Jones best describes an air-cooled charging system and the recommended replacement parts.

Those adventurers planning to ride fully loaded touring bikes around the world off-road (as well as on) should consider strengthening their suspension systems. Methods include the addition of a fork brace and frame support pieces, the upgrading of springs and shocks, and the reinforcement of frame welds.

In general, replace all tired or suspicious cables, rubber, and wires. Before beginning any long ride, invest in a new set of tubes and tires. If you're planning for the worst possible riding conditions, a common mistake is to start with expensive off-road tires. I made that mistake once, only to discover that long before I arrived at the point where I would need them for off-roading, the regular interstate and pavement I took to get there had burned them up. With this lesson in mind, on my Kawasaki project bike I did begin crossing Russia with the hardest road tires I could find, knowing that most of the next 10,000 miles would be on pavement. What little off-road mileage I'd clock would be fine at slow speed.

Protection

On the long ride around the world, riders face weather and road conditions of all kinds. They and their bikes need as much protection as possible from elements, such as water and wind, as well as from spills and crashes. Measures for improving protection can include mounting a higher windshield, adding hand-lever guards, and attaching mudguards. Radiator and water pump guards offer motorcycles greater protection in the event of a sideways fall or a front-end collision.

Outfitting My BMW and Kawasaki

Two motorcycles I've prepared for world rides are the BMW G/S, an older model with low mileage when I started, and a new Kawasaki KLR, practically fresh out of the box. Both took me to the ends of the earth. Since both motorcycles were nearly stock, I had to make many additions.

Outfitting My BMW for a Global Ride

A popular misconception about the BMW GS is that you can purchase a good, used R80 or R100GS for a reasonable price and immediately take off and ride it smoothly around the world. In reality, the chances of having a mechanically uneventful global romp aboard either stock bike are slim. Although BMW's highly popular enduro model has become legendary for its world conquests, my experience after four rides around the globe is that I have seen and heard proportionately more about broken BMWs than about any other model. I fondly tell people that my BMWs have left me stranded in some of the worst places on the planet! Several of those strandings were due to mechanical failures that couldn't have been foreseen; others were problems that could have been prevented by more careful preparation.

Outfitting a BMW is fairly similar to outfitting any other bike for a long trip. When I equipped my R100GS, I opted to add a 43-liter plastic tank to my motorcycle for a couple of reasons. I wanted the added fuel capacity—twice that of the stock tank—and the lower center of gravity. The price of the aftermarket tank, with the mounting system, was about $750. I could have had a stock, slightly used BMW tank with greater fuel capacity, the Paris-to-Dakar metal model, for about $700, but the benefits of the larger plastic tank over the stock metal tank were worth the extra $50.

Next, I added a rear luggage rack, something to tie a couple of waterproof bags to. Then I added tank and seat panniers. My favorite tank and seat panniers, offered through Aerostich/Riderwearhouse, come in two sizes; you can also get them waterproofed. I prefer the larger model, which mounts with a set of Velcro straps and bungee cords and allows you to carry items in easy-to-reach places but out of sight of any curious onlookers.

I carry tools, spare inner tubes, and drinking water in the two panniers that hang over the gas tank. Filled, they also serve as wind and water protection and have, on several occasions,

In Africa I found the desert riding fun, often being off the pavement for days at a time.

A young Moroccan imagines himself riding the world. I am a sucker for kids who want to sit on my bike and gave this one a ride through his village atop my luggage. We were the entertainment for the week.

absorbed the hit my knee would have taken after a slight get-off. I store my cameras and some clothing in the two panniers I mount under the seat and behind my legs. To support the weight of added tools and other heavier items, I make sure the panniers are resting on top of the rear foot pegs.

I added a tank bag next. Deciding to use a plastic gas tank precluded the use of any bags that attached magnetically. Since I had already chose to add the larger gas tank, certain bags were ruled out—especially the generic ones manufacturers design to conform to as many tanks as possible. The steep angle of the 43-liter gas tank made several of the generic models unusable. Fortunately, there is a wide range of tank bags on the market; in fact, I've

used several brands. I like a bag that expands to close to 40 liters. My personal choice is the Wolfman Explorer bag, which is smaller than my old favorite, the Harro bag from Germany. It costs about half what other bags cost and is readily available.

Next, as usual, I got rid of the stock seat since sitting on one of those is about as comfortable as sitting on a 2 × 12 inch board. To replace it, I hand fitted an aftermarket seat to the stock base.

Then I added a handlebar-mounted windshield system, which cost less than $100. While the windshield I selected was not the manufacturer's plastic, and it certainly did not match the advertising images of slipstreaming desert winds, it did cut twice the wind

The clutch splines on this BMW went farther south than did the bike, so we're loading it onto a truck for the final 100 miles to Ushuaia, Argentina. There we put in a second-hand plate, and the rider continued on around South America.

at a third of the cost. Some companies (including Touratech) offer hand-lever guards, and I decided to buy a pair. These provide not only wind and water protection, but also insurance against a broken BMW lever mount, which would easily cost me twice what I paid for the guards.

I took off the stock side panels and replaced them with plastic mudguards from an auto supply house. When I did this, I attached them to the motorcycle frame with cable ties fed through holes I drilled. You'll find that on long-distance trips, some form of side panel is needed to keep the water off the rear wheel from flying up to the tops of your boots. In addition, the mudguards will give some backing to the

side panniers that are resting on the tops of the rear foot pegs.

When I prepped my motorcycle, the first electrical part I changed was the rotor, which is the part that most often goes bad. I replaced it with a rotor from Motorrad Elektrik. This model is about one-third the price of the original BMW part, and, according to Rick Jones, is built with better winding and glue.

While I was under the front cover changing the rotor, I also replaced the stock diode board with one designed for better cooling, less vibration, and superior grounding. This unit is the part second most prone to failure.

Because the 1981 model is one of the "prefix" models, I also replaced the output regulator, bumping the stock output from 13.8 to 14.2 volts. This is necessary for a more complete charging of the battery.

While the gas tank was off, I replaced the ignition coil; the original coil was known to crack and die over time from heat. If you're using a stock BMW coil for a replacement, then the ignition module must also be replaced at the same time. I used a Motorrad Elektrik coil, and while I was at it, I installed one of Motorrad's replacement ignition modules. By replacing the original BMW equipment using aftermarket parts, I saved more than $200 for both units.

As usual, I replaced the bike's battery. For this particular project, I chose a sealed gel battery from Motorrad Elektrik. It's maintenance free, and it will not leak if the motorcycle is turned on its side or upended.

In addition, I replaced all of the bike's lights.

The final component to be replaced was the Hall sender unit controlling the spark timing. Over time, this unit can fail due to heat; if failure occurs, the unit cannot be repaired by the side of the road. While changing the Hall unit, I also changed both spark plugs and wires.

I gave some thought to replacing the electric starter. If the motorcycle had only had an electric starter, I would have made this change. But because this bike had less than 10,000 miles on it and had a kick-starter, I chose to leave the unit alone. I recommend that newer starters, such as the French-made Veleo model, be replaced because typically original starters are known to be unreliable and, in the case of the newer GS models, the bike does not come with a kick-starter.

About half of one of the panniers on my R80 G/S is filled with spare parts and tools.

This motorcyclist traveling through India has factory boxes on his BMW. Knowing they leaked, he simply avoided riding in the rain.

To toughen the suspension, I added a fork brace and Progressive Fork springs. The combination gave the front end the needed stiffness to support the heavier weight of a fully loaded touring bike, whether on-road or off-road.

I considered upgrading the rear suspension. The motorcycle I was preparing for this project was a reasonably new one (in terms of number of miles), but it had a reputation for blowing seals or breaking, so I upgraded to an aftermarket rear shock rather than use an OEM new shock. The aftermarket rear shock—and there are several makes available—is usually stronger and less prone to blowing seals. Even if this should happen, this shock can be rebuilt, whereas the OEM part cannot be.

The early model GS frame, particularly the rear subframe, has been known to crack, especially under the touring weight stress. For my bike, I welded supporting pieces along the parts known to break and strengthened the frame welds. Germany's HPN Company offers a full frame kit.

To lighten the motorcycle, I gutted the muffler and removed the pollution control plumbing. Both changes were legal in the places on the globe where I was taking the motorcycle. I also relocated the front and rear turn signals. In their original locations, they could have easily broken off. The original air cleaner was replaced with a reusable one so I would not have to carry a spare with me or worry about finding a replacement in my travels.

Since the GS transmission is known to break, I sent it out for a complete rebuild and had a "shift-kit" installed as well. While the transmission was out, I checked the clutch plate and spring for wear. My bike had low mileage, so neither part was changed, but if it had experienced hard use or had high mileage (40,000–50,000), I would have changed the clutch plate, mainly because it's easy to do at this stage when the transmission is out.

I also invested in new tires and tubes and clutch, brake, and gas cables. The choke cables were checked but didn't need replacing. The BMW was now ready for a long ride around the world!

Preparing a Kawasaki for Global Travel

To get the Kawasaki prepared for my fourth global trip, I enlisted the help of a group of knowledgeable and energetic consultants from the KLR Internet group sponsored by Dual Sport News and from "Mr. KLR," also known as Elden Carl, of El Cajon, California. Working with them, as well as recruiting some outside help from sponsors and advisers, I prepared the KLR for its world ride.

Because the motorcycle was going out of the United States, I removed some of the evaporative emissions equipment. This minimized the plumbing and lightened the starting weight while still meeting the pollution standards of my home state, as well as those of Russia and Africa. Next, I disconnected the side stand cutout switch because it was known to be vulnerable to mud and water and could kill the engine if it malfunctioned.

The rear license plate I moved up on the back fender because in its original position, the plate could make contact with the rear wheel in severe bumps. If this happened, it could bend or rip off. Repositioned higher under the license plate light, it was safe and well lit. I secured it with locking fasteners and a small padlock. The lock would lessen the chance of the plate being removed by souvenir seekers who attach significance to U.S. license plates, a cool collector's item in some cultures.

The KLR comes with a satisfactory electrical system. However, since I wanted to make a few minor changes, I was concerned about overburdening the charging system, especially at low rpm. I installed an aftermarket accessory socket so I could plug in an electric jacket liner from Aerostich to fit into my Aerostich Darien riding suit. (I wanted to keep warm in frosty climes!) While the socket itself drew no power, the liner was rated at 70 watts. However, the KLR alternator was estimated to put out only 200 watts. Ordinarily, this is enough wattage to keep things working and the battery charged, but not with the liner on "cook," especially at low rpm. So I installed a higher output stator (275 watts) from Electrix USA, with a sturdier regulator, designed to pump out the extra amperes needed.

Next, I added a switch to the headlight system to shut off the light while the motorcycle was running. This is not legal in the United States or in most of Europe, but in many parts of the world, driving with the light on actually works against the motorcyclist by bringing unwanted attention from oncoming drivers. In these places, such as India and Africa, motorcyclists don't usually drive with their headlights on during daylight hours, the popular belief being that having the light on increases gas consumption. As a result, oncoming drivers think that you do not know your light is on, so they frantically signal you with flashing headlights and try waving you down.

I next replaced the rear taillight with a heavy-duty one supplied by Dual Star, a company specializing in parts, designs, and modifications to motorcycles such as the KLR. The new light had thicker filaments, which made it less susceptible to breaking from vibration.

Ready for a 19,631-mile ride around the world, the single cylinder 650cc Kawasaki was to be my home as I crossed 24 time zones.

HEADLIGHT
SHIELD

Headlights can be expensive (some more than $200!) and hard to find. Try a StonGard headlight shield over the glass to protect it from flying rocks and debris. It isn't a bad idea to use one when riding around near home either.

The final electrical modification I made was to change the original battery to a sealed unit, which I purchased from Battery-Web (at http://www.battery-web.com). Thinking of the inevitable "upside-down scenario," I opted for a maintenance-free and nonspillable battery. While I was under the seat installing the battery, I rerouted several wires and secured them with cable ties to prevent chafing.

I briefly considered replacing the fuses with more robust types, then relocating the holder, but this meant I'd have to cut into the existing wiring system. Likewise, I'd have to do this if I changed the headlight to a higher output bulb. I decided against both options because I have learned that splicing wires increases the number of places where things can go wrong. Instead, I left much of the stock wiring in place and followed the well-known motorcycle adventurer's adage: never ride at night. (I also carried a few extra fuses!)

The 6.1-gallon fuel capacity of the KLR provided a range of nearly 300 miles, depending on speed, so I stayed with the stock tank knowing that, throughout most of the world, gasoline can be found easily within a radius of 200–250 miles. For those places where gasoline might not be readily available, I figured I could always add an inexpensive plastic gas tank to the back or carry it in my side pannier and discard it when I returned to places with gas stations. I didn't see any reason for purchasing a larger gas tank (which would cost me an additional $500), when I would use it only one or twice. Instead, I would invest $10 or less on a small disposable plastic container.

Kawasaki has been tweaking the KLR 650 engine since 1987, but there is still one spring whose malfunction can cause the engine to grenade. This small spring, called the balancer lever adjuster spring, has been known to break. I didn't want something like this to happen to me while I was crossing Russia, which requires visitors to submit a fixed itinerary with entrance and exit dates to receive their visas. Waiting for several weeks while parts—or an entire engine—were flown in would throw me way off schedule. In addition, my travel funds would take a significant hit if I had to pay for major repairs. As insurance against these problems, I decided to take some precautions.

The rider should adjust the balancer chain every 3,000 miles. However, if you're making this adjustment and you don't notice that the adjuster spring has broken it can be disastrous! The tensioner can be pulled backward by the weight of the chain instead of forward, where it is tightened by the small spring. This causes slack in the balancer chain, which can, in turn, jump off its gears. Once the balancer chain is off the gears, several

MOSCOW

things can happen, including bent valves and irreparable damage to the engine case. With this in mind, always be sure the spring is still in one piece and attached to its two holding points before loosening the tensioner bolt. If the spring is broken or disconnected, the motorcycle may still be operable, but it won't run perfectly. You may be able to get it to a shop where the spring can be replaced, but it's always preferable not to get into that situation in the first place.

Elden Carl and Scott Wexman, both of San Diego, California, came up with a unique way of checking to see if the spring is in place. Their fix is called a "balance spring inspection window." By drilling a hole through the inner rotor/balancer cover at the lower mounting bolt hole (directly in front of the adjuster spring), an inspection can be made each time you adjust the balancer chain. If the spring is in place, then the tensioner bolt can be loosened to allow for adjustment. If the spring is flopping around or missing, then the tensioner bolt should be left tightened and the motorcycle ridden to a place where the repair can be made.

This drilled-hole procedure can save thousands of dollars in a complete engine rebuild and weeks spent waiting for parts. While making this modification can take a couple of hours, in addition to a special alignment bolt and nylon washer, the time investment is well worth the insurance against disaster.

An aftermarket "fix" for this problem has since been designed—a heavier replacement spring as well as a one-piece balancer idler shaft lever (it was formerly several pieces welded

TIPS ABOUT PANNIERS

Aluminum panniers are not bulletproof or theftproof. They do not ensure the security of things locked inside, even with an integrated locking system. A determined thief can get into any aluminum pannier, often as quickly as he can get into an OEM plastic saddlebag.

How the aluminum pannier mounts to the motorcycle is a major consideration. Some systems are sold with their own motorcycle-specific mounting racks, while others are kits in which a basic box fits on several different racks. For instance, Happy Trails Products makes several mounting systems—for a Kawasaki KLR or a BMW F650GS—and its Pannier Mount Kit allows panniers to be moved back and forth between the two motorcycles.

Another consideration is the cradle mount versus the flush mount system. In one case, the aluminum pannier bolts mount or affix to a flush frame; in the other, the pannier sits on top of a holder that is part of the mounting rack and is then attached to the holder at the base and sides.

Happy Trails Products and Touratech offer a "puck system" for attaching panniers to the frames. The puck is hardened plastic in the shape of a hockey puck. It is used at two or four of the corners to support weight in a flush frame on the back. Each allows for a quick "easy-on/off" system so the pannier is not dependent upon the locks, clamps, or clips used by other integrated systems.

• Aluminum leaves black marks against light objects like cloth, paper, and plastic. I glue linoleum to the inside of my aluminum panniers, while others use bag liners (although storage space is lost with this method). Some panniers are powder-coated. Both bag liners and powder-coating cost a little more.

This is one way to test whether your bags are waterproof, but I don't recommend it. A small crash landed me in the stream.

- I prefer a hinged top to a removable top. While I have not yet lost a top, I know others who have. Always spend extra time making sure that the removable tops are clamped down securely.

- If you're using a hinged top box, pick the box with the hinge on the outside rather than against the seat. This lets the top open into a small "table." You might also consider a hinged top that folds completely forward or backward, forward being best when luggage is strapped to the back.

- Make sure one of the two panniers is wide enough to accommodate a helmet. It's safer than leaving your helmet hanging by the chinstrap where someone will be tempted to make off with it while you are doing a little sightseeing.

- Allow for a ten-millimeter space between the top of the box and the top of the seat for your passenger's legs.

- The OEM mounting system (frames) will probably not support the aluminum panniers and additional weight. Generally, aluminum panniers carry more than the stock luggage system—"more" translating into more weight. While you can make do with the OEM mounts on a short run— and maybe add additional strength by

gusseting—eventually you will experience breakage, especially if you're going off-road or into rugged terrain.

- The cheapest box is not the best deal. The most inexpensive boxes on the market cost around $200 for a set. However, at one-millimeter thick, they cannot be bolted to frames because the sides are paper-thin. When I used boxes this thin, I had to rivet another two-millimeter plate to the inside wall to get the needed support. Even then, when the motorcycle tipped over, the box crumpled.

- Purchasing the priciest system does not ensure the best quality either. One traveler I met in Alaska had a set of the most expensive aluminum panniers he could purchase. He said that from day one they leaked. Eventually, he drilled holes in the bottom of each so the water would run out!

- I prefer aluminum boxes that allow the bike to pass through an open American-size doorway or through the entrance of a Central American hotel (where they often insist you park for the night) when fitted to the motorcycle.

- If the box and mounting system are likely to bend, or break when the motorcycle is placed on its side, do not use them. Yet you do not want something constructed of bridge-building material either. Choose a pannier that you can repair without having to send it back to the manufacturer.

- Depending on the motorcycle, standard panniers usually work fine. Several manufacturers can custom-make a system for you, but delivery time will take longer and they'll cost more.

together and thus subject to breakage). This fix is fondly referred to as a "doohicky" and my local Kawasaki dealer charges $150 for installation and parts. If these two pieces are installed, then the inspection hole modification is not necessary. Either way, however, some work is needed under the cover in order to address the springtensioner problem.

I made other changes, as well. For example, I installed a fuel filter to work with the Tygon fuel line. I did this to prevent particles from reaching the carburetor and to make sure the fuel line didn't crack from "unsavory" gas. Additionally, I installed a reusable air and oil filters from Dual

Star, because I didn't want to carry spares. I also changed the spark plug to an NGK DPR8EVX-9 model, reputed to give a stronger—but not hotter—spark.

Other than a valve adjustment and the addition of a magnetized and lower profile oil drain plug, no additional alterations were made to the engine, transmission, intake, or exhaust systems.

For suspension changes, I went to Precision Concepts in El Cajon, California, where a set of Progressive fork springs were put in the front forks. In addition, the shop anodized the fork legs, hardening them and reducing stiction. A small hole in the inner tube was

Prepare your bike for all conditions, including roads such as this South American one.

opened to a 1/16-inch hole for better rebound dampening. Then the forks were reassembled and shimmed at the axle to ensure straightness.

On the rear end, I installed a Progressive Suspension Larry Roeseler Signature 420 Series shock absorber. A bit of grinding on the swing arm was required because of the increased thickness of the spring. A 4-inch-wide rubber flap was fashioned and installed between the swing arm and the rear fender. This kept sand, rocks, and water from being thrown forward onto the unprotected piston rod of the shock absorber.

The KLR 650 does not come with a center stand, but this is something I wanted in order to simplify chain adjustment and rear wheel removal. It would also be helpful when I parked, especially on ferryboats or during transport. I again went to the "one-stop KLR shop," Dual Star, for the stand it manufactures. The center stand bolted right on, with no modifications needed.

Since I was rapidly adding weight to the bike, I had to give some thought to the rear subframe and possible breakage at the three mounting points. Again Dual Star had the fix—a complete subframe bolt kit filled with extra-strength bolts and the drill bits needed to install them.

I decided to replace all of the softer nuts, bolts, and screws with stronger or stainless steel ones from the Sagebrush Machine Shop. Its mail order kit replaces everything from handlebar control bolts to the front brake reservoir screws.

Needing sturdy and lockable saddlebags, I selected the aluminum pan-

To check the suspension on the Hartford in Taiwan, I am riding it through some snake grass. Since I hate snakes, I spent more time looking for them than watching out for ruts or holes.

niers and mounting system from Happy Trails Products. These were designed specifically for the KLR 650 and mounted easily to the frame. I also added Happy Trails' turn signal mounts, which allowed me to use the existing turn signals and wiring. Though I used its standard product, Happy Trails also offers customization of the width and height of the aluminum panniers.

For tank panniers, I opted for the waterproofed Aerostich ones. They mount across the top of the gas tank with a system of Velcro straps and bungee cords that connect to the lower corners. Initially, I installed the tank panniers on the gas tank but eventually moved them so they were suspended over the frame (under the seat). They rested on top of the rear passenger foot pegs in front of the aluminum panniers.

To protect various points on the motorcycle engine, I discarded the Kawasaki plastic bash plate and replaced it with an aluminum skid plate from D. H. Gibbs and Company. Gibbs has been manufacturing and fine-tuning the KLR 650 skid plate for nearly fifteen years and supplies most of the skid plates in the KLR market. It bolts right on and leaves enough air between itself and the engine to ensure that no rubbing occurs.

For wind protection, I bolted on a taller windshield available from Kawasaki, opting for the smoked version. I then installed a set of Dual Star hand-lever guards with wind spoilers. At the same time, I discarded the hard factory handgrips in favor of a pair of more comfortable Progrip ones. I adjusted the setting of the handlebars;

this was not only for better rider position but also to avoid hitting the larger windshield with the mirrors at full lock. Then I installed a brake master cylinder guard (also from Dual Star), a sturdier brake pedal mount, water pump guard, and clear headlight protector. While I was installing the brake pedal mount, I noticed that the original factory setting and positioning marks on the brake lever allowed the pedal to rub the engine case. Fortunately, when I made a two-mark adjustment to the lever's position, the rubbing stopped without affecting the rear brake tension.

A potential problem on the KLR 650 is radiator fan damage if the motorcycle falls on its left side. The fan shroud can be pushed onto the plastic fan blades, causing them to break. However, Dual Star has the fix for this problem with their radiator guard, which bolts right on. Another potential damage point with a left-side fall is the shift lever, which has been known to bend inward and crack the engine case. I bolted on a much stronger shift lever, again from Dual Star.

Not surprisingly, the stock seat is a butt-buster. It is fine for short hops, but hard as a board on longer rides. So I took the stock seat to NBI Upholstery in San Diego, which quickly transformed it by giving it a wider, softer base, and a new cover. NBI makes its modifications after considering the height, the inseam, and the weight of the rider.

Warnings of speedometer failure prompted me to order a speedometer cable (a shorter cable drive) from Dual Star. While I was on the Dual Star Web site, I ordered Fuji-Lock nuts for the front and rear axles. I needed to compensate for the increased weight of the motorcycle; I also wanted to improve the lower end pulling power. So I changed the rear sprocket to one with forty-four teeth. While the rear wheel was off, I added a DID chain with a riveted master link.

To gain maximum wear from the new sprocket and chain, I installed a TK 7 Scottoiler, which I purchased from ActionStations. The added mileage from two chains and sprockets would compensate for the cost of the items and I wouldn't have to hunt for replacements if I were somewhere in the middle of Siberia.

The KLR 650 comes with a tool kit, but it's a "mini" and I wanted to add some items, such as tire irons, sockets, longer wrenches, cable tires, wire, and feeler gauges. I contacted BMR Bike Bags (in Colorado), and they got me off to a good start with their Toolshed tool pouch, big enough to hold everything I wanted to add. In addition to the KLR tool kit, Dual Star's Tool Works kit easily fits into the Toolshed. To this, I added an array of tools and small items, eventually filling the Toolshed with everything that I would need on my ride. I stored the Toolshed in one of the lower Aerostich tank panniers, in order to keep the center of gravity low.

At this point, I was ready for a test ride. I needed to see which changes worked, which ones didn't, and what modifications I still needed to make. The first leg of my world ride was across North America. This is an easy ride because it's mostly on interstates with some off-roading in Montana and Colorado. The miles are easy, and

you can achieve speeds in the 70-mph range on the highway.

After the trip across North America and before I stuffed the KLR into a shipping container in Florida, I made a few necessary last-minute changes. Dual Star sent me a radiator guard that included an opposite side-mounted water pump guard; both pieces were triangulated and stronger than the previously installed guards. The system bolted onto the frame neck and lower engine mounts, which offered superior protection not only from a sideways fall but also from a front hit. I bolted it on for insurance.

At the same time, I added Dual Star's Magura Hydraulic Clutch Kit. This would lower the clutch pull from between 25 and 35 pounds to 15. It also would increase the usable clutch engagement figuring to lower fatigue, especially in the slow speed work I'd encounter in Sahara sands.

The last add-on was a billet oil filter cap installed to keep people from adding foreign substances to the engine oil. The stock plastic cap was easily removable, but this one came with a small wrench that fit on my key ring. For carrying capacity (for things like a tent, sleeping bag, and air mattress), I added the Wolfman Alfa Rear Bag with side packs and a large dry duffel from Riderwearhouse to shelter items that need to be protected from water. A couple extra heavy-duty bungee cords secured everything to the back of the bike. Partway through my trip, I reached Germany and looked at the Avon Distanzias tires. They were fine, but the rear had two holes from foreign objects I had picked up in

The owner of this Triumph is about to try for 10,000 plus miles in ten days in the 2003 Iron Butt Rally. That's about halfway around the world in land miles (most on pavement). In general, the bike's a bit over-prepared for me, but I would have opted for more wind protection.

Africa. Rather than risk not finding a compatible set of tires in Russia, I installed two "rock hard" Avon Roadrunners. I knew that 90 percent of the ride ahead was on pavement as I was going to cross eight time zones on the way to eastern Russia. The other 10 percent was going to be through mud, easily filling up a knobby, so any dual-sport tire would be as useless as the Roadrunners. Slow going with the Roadrunners would offset having to carry knobbies for those small sections, so I picked up knobbies before heading to Russia.

The Monster Tubes from Dual Star did their job when I got a puncture in Morocco, causing a slow leak. (A thinner tube would have gone flat well before I reached a town.) A second puncture in deep sand kept the air from escaping quickly allowing me to ride on the leaking tube to a flat spot where repairs could be made.

The radiator guard I installed paid off when I rode on a high-speed gravel road in the Sahara Desert. Cresting the top, four sleeping camels stood up. Rather than plow through the dromedaries, I veered off into a ditch, the sand eating the front wheel. The motorcycle went down on its left side. The radiator guard took the hit from the front, protecting the fragile shroud and plastic fan blades.

The Happy Trails aluminum panniers proved their worth in more extreme conditions than just rain (where they kept everything dry). An errant driver speeding through a traffic circle hit the right pannier from behind. The aluminum pannier took the hit, with the mounting system absorbing some of the impact. If there had been no give in the pannier mounts, the impact would have been more abrupt, and the motorcycle would have gone to the pavement.

After loosening the mounts, adjusting the box, and tightening it up again, the only damage was a small dent. However, if I had been using plastic panniers, they would have shattered or split upon impact.

The aftermarket DID chain made the entire trip—all 19,631 miles—as

Near China I stopped to help the rider of a broken down Ural (right).

did both sprockets, in part due to the Scottoiler and to regular maintenance. Only one adjustment to the tensioners was needed on my trip.

The KLR never missed a beat, even when I mistakenly loaded 80-octane petrol in Russia. While I had some concern about valve adjustments being

needed at the three-quarters point (Germany), an inspection proved that everything was within specifications and no adjustments were necessary. Other than changing the oil, the Kawasaki proved to be maintenance-free for the entire global ride.

I did learn some things about the Kawasaki. For example, the modification to the stock seat was not drastic enough. I would have preferred a softer "bucket style" seat to the harder bench I used. (I kept the bench style, thinking that I might want to put someone on the back, but this never happened.) A single bucket seat, composed of softer foam, would have made my 400- to 500-mile days more enjoyable.

I spent less time at speeds above 60 mph than planned, so the taller windshield I had added was still too low and this caused buffeting. Instead of using the nine-inch aftermarket windscreen, I should have chosen the eleven-inch model, but this choice would have required adding structural support to the fairing pod.

Somewhere in Siberia, my relocated license plate disappeared; I still don't know if it was from vibration or tampering. On closer inspection, the plastic fender had cracked, but what caused the cracking—human hands or bumpy roads—I couldn't tell.

Today, the KLR is sitting in my studio, resting. It has made only a few short trips since that long ride. I believe with a fresh set of tires, new chain and sprockets, an oil change, and a valve check, it would be ready for another global ride. Throw in a new seat and taller windscreen—and a bucket of money—and I might go with it.

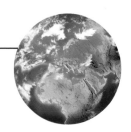

RIDER PREPARATION

hile riding around the world is much easier today than in the past, it still takes time, money, careful planning, and mental and physical preparation. How much money you budget on your ride depends on how long you plan to be gone and what type of lifestyle you plan on maintaining while on the road. One American couple spent somewhere between $250,000 and $300,000 on their ride around the world. At the other end of the scale, there are those riders who claim to have spent only about $10 per day. For a two-year tour, that's less than $7,500. A whopping difference! Obviously, the well-heeled couple slept in five-star hotels while the low-end travelers camped behind gas stations.

As you travel, your habits will have to change. You need to adjust your lifestyle because the rest of the world will not adjust to you. I am surprised when I hear Western travelers, especially Americans, complaining about lifestyles in foreign countries. Isn't the reason for leaving home on a trip like this to experience the rest of the world, not to find fault with others for failing to adapt to Western styles or habits?

Preparing a Budget

Most of us don't have hundreds of thousands of dollars to spend on a ride. That means it's important to carefully budget our money. One of the biggest mistakes you can make when planning for a 'round-the-world ride is to spend too much on the front-end preparation, leaving less for the ride itself. When this happens, riders usually end up shortening the trip. To avoid that fate, keep in mind as you prepare that the big front-end expenditures should be for the motorcycle itself and outfitting it with essentials. Though it is tempting, don't throw thousands of dollars into unnecessary accessories, the ones you'll never really need. For instance, while accessory lighting looks good on your bike and gives you more light, you should be following the rider's cardinal rule—Never Ride at Night. So why would you need it? (Surprisingly, most modern motorcycles have adequate lighting systems when the bike is used cautiously, meaning at a slower speed and during daylight. Remember, if you are on a global ride, you are not in a race with time—unless you're trying to set a record.)

One rider I know purchased a new BMW, then spent as much on accessories as he did for the motorcycle. After adding the cost of his riding suit, helmet, and computerized electronic gizmos, he had invested more on his equipment than he had on the guide for his tour around the world. Unfortunately for him, he crashed on the first day out of the box—both he and his expensively outfitted motorcycle came home on an airplane.

Cost Differences Among Countries

On my fourth ride around the world, my expenses averaged between $2,000

Bring a big wallet when riding in Japan. Toll roads, which abound, were about 25 cents per mile when I was there last.

and $3,000 per month over the five months I was on the road. While crossing Europe, my expenses were on the high end, nearly $200 per day: approximately $75 per day for gas, tolls, and oil; nearly $50 for sleeping; and the rest for food, insurance, and bike maintenance. Once I got to Russia, my daily price dropped because I was able to sleep and eat inexpensively and gas was closer to $20 per day.

In 1997, I budgeted $25 per day to ride from North America to the bottom of South America. My actual costs turned out to be $35 per day. I hadn't realized how expensive things were in some South American countries, especially costs associated with crossing borders and shipping my bike over impassable, or nearly impassable, sections such as the Darien Gap.

Without a doubt, the most expensive country I have traveled in is Japan. Travel there cost, easily, $200 per day—and that was eating at 7-Elevens. After I factored in the price of getting to Japan, insurance, and handling, I wished I were back in Bolivia or India, where travel was about a quarter of the cost.

Calculating the Costs

When I am preparing for my trip, I work out a budget for everything I foresee as a travel expense associated with the journey, including costs that continue at home while I am away, such as telephone, taxes, and utilities. After computing the actual hard costs for the trip, I add 40 percent for unplanned expenses, such as an evening on the town or an emergency, and for small items such film, postage, and souvenirs. Once I arrive at the

---

COMPUTING DAILY EXPENSES

For computing daily travel expenses, I use a simple table for each country:

Gas/Oil	.$
Food	+ $ _____
Sleeping	+ $ _____
Total Per Day	= $ _____
Number of days in country	X _____
Total Daily Cost	= $ _____

Besides the daily travel allowance, other factors you should not overlook when budgeting include:

- health insurance while traveling
- airfare/sea passage in and out of countries for motorcycle and rider
- crating (if required) at an average cost of $200 to $500
- border crossing costs
- handler fees
- Carnet de Passages en Douane (a type of motor vehicle touring permit required in some countries)
- motorcycle insurance, sometimes re-quired from country to country
- tires, maintenance, and spare parts
- Internet/telephone/fax (Internet can range from $1 to $18 per hour)
- laundry
- money handling (some countries charge 3 percent or more for cashing traveler's checks, and in the Philippines, each ATM transaction cost me $45, no matter the amount of the withdrawal)
- miscellaneous (the great "unknowns," such as emergency airfare home, motorcycle repairs, replacement of lost/stolen items like cameras, laptops, GPSs, credit cards, passports, and emergency medical care on the road, which your travel insurance doesn't cover)

Life moves at different paces and in different ways all over the world. You'll find places where the horse and cart are still the main form of transportation.

adjusted hard costs, I add my preparation expenses, which include the cost of the motorcycle, accessories added or waiting to be added, and my riding gear. Once I have computed these trip costs, I look at my budget and determine how long my ride can be.

Of course, there are exceptions to this formula. For example, you may start out with a plan, then decide to stop and make money along the way to stretch out your trip. Or you may opt to fly home and make more money, then return to the road. There are riders who run out of money and borrow from friends and family; and there are riders who beg their way across the continents. (The beggars send out e-mails to lists they have developed of friends and supporters or motorcycle groups, recounting sad stories of woe, asking for funds to be deposited to their accounts. Another ploy is to use motorcycle brand club directories for free places to stay since the directories list contact information. The Internet has moved this into a cyber business with some travelers using PayPal accounts for credit card deposits.)

I do not favor any of those options. I prefer to arrive at a budget and live within it for the duration of my trip. Yet unexpected expenses do crop up. Frequently, I have been surprised by the actual cost of a trip. One trip, which I initially figured to cost $1,500 per month, actually ended up being nearly three times that when I had to change motorcycles mid-trip. This included the cost of returning to the United States to sell a vehicle for more funds. However, had I not gone back and sold the vehicle, I would have found myself on that dreaded sand-eating, motorcycle-pushing tour of Africa.

As a starting point for estimating country costs, I consult travel guides such as those from the Lonely Planet. These give me an idea of how much it will cost to get into a country as well as room and food costs. From there I try to find a "biker friendly" contact in the country, or someone familiar with travel through that country, to query for information regarding items such as gas prices, insurance, and general travel costs.

Lifestyle Changes

Your lifestyle is going to change as soon as you leave on your long ride. Everything—from your sleeping habits to your choice of food—is going to be different. If you are a pizza-and-beer type of eater and refuse to eat anything else, you are going to be hungry across Africa or India. If you are a steak-and-eggs breakfast person, you'll soon be disappointed when you discover that the rest of the world does not enjoy huge American-style breakfasts. Those two morning cups of coffee you need each day will set you back much more in Germany than in the States, and there are seldom free refills.

If you're tall and traveling through Asia, you'll find your feet hanging over the end of the bed. Outside the United States, you'll seldom find a washcloth in your bathroom. In certain regions, you're not likely to find a sitting toilet; instead, there will be a squatter, a porcelain platform at floor level with a hole in the middle for a target. Toilet paper can be at a premium. Learn to carry a supply with you at all times. Sometimes it can be purchased at the entrance to a public restroom from a vendor or vending machine. Often, there will be nothing, especially in gas stations in developing countries.

In preparation for an overseas trip, make sure you allow enough time for a passport to be processed and to determine whether visas, vaccines, or other special arrangements are needed. Also keep in mind that in any country you travel through, the U.S. embassy will not serve as your safety net in case of disaster. While an official may visit you if you find yourself in jail, the assistance is usually limited to matters concerning your passport (replacing it if lost or stolen or getting additional pages added) and possibly advice on what to do or who to contact if

Usually, I prefer to go it alone but when I met this young woman in Cuba, I did offer room on the back of my motorcycle if she wanted to travel with me on the rest of my ride around the world.

problems arise. I once had to get a letter of permission to purchase a motorcycle in a foreign country from the embassy, which they provided to me once I gave them wording needed. There was no cost for the letter. The embassy, or consulate, is 90 percent a political entity for the U.S. government and 10 percent a service provider for U.S. citizens. If you lose your money and credit cards, do not expect a loan or grant from the embassy. Have a better back-up plan in those cases, as well as for hospital care.

In case of medical emergency, I have always been a "cash-and-carry" traveler for small matters while making sure my HMO policy remains paid up and in effect back home. If I need new eyeglasses on the road, I purchase them out of pocket. I do the same with shots, prescription drugs, or visits to a physician. Some travelers choose to pay for additional travel insurance or medical evacuation insurance to get them back home if they have an accident ($150–$250). I would recommend that everyone purchase whatever level of insurance makes them feel comfortable.

Before leaving on one of my long trips, I mentally prepare myself for the changes ahead by starting to look at how I live, and then trying to anticipate how that lifestyle is going to change. For instance, I quit drinking coffee. On the road coffee is often expensive and—when I can find it—unsatisfactory in taste.

Washing clothes, or having them washed for you, is always a challenge. When I was in Monaco, I couldn't find

German friend Doris Wiedemann, like me, prefers riding solo and has covered most of the world with only her bike for company.

a Laundromat. Returning to the hotel, I asked the front desk where I could find one, and the receptionist stuffily stated, "In Monaco, there are no Laundromats." It was as if doing your own laundry was beneath the dignity of the average Monaco resident. I later found out that all laundry should be left with the hotel clerk and it would be sent out to be done. Buying a beer in a Muslim country is not as easy as walking to the corner bar or over to the 7-Eleven. Several times, I found myself standing in a back alley, buying a beer on the black market.

My biggest challenge is to mentally prepare myself to think outside of my personal box when it comes to problem-solving. For example, when I needed a tire in Mozambique, I had to face the reality that I was not going to find the exact size and style I had been using on my motorcycle. What finally settled on was the only tire in town that would fit my rim. Although it was smaller, and made for dirt, it was all that was available.

There are travelers who insist on using special tires because they think they are the only ones that will work on their motorcycles. Once I had to send a set of German tires to a rider who was stuck in Colombia because all she was familiar with were the tires recommended by the manufacturer of her motorcycle. The tires, including shipping and import duties, ended up costing more than twice as much as they should have. Meanwhile, a set of locally manufactured or cheaper tires would have saved her two weeks of waiting time, and she would have had money to buy another set sometime down the road.

PREPARE FOR THE WORST

- Medical insurance or travel insurance should include an evacuation clause.
- Learn cardiopulmonary resuscitation (CPR) before you go—you may meet someone along the way who needs it.
- Talk to your doctor.

I should have been wearing my helmet when I took this ride through Africa. The bird kept trying to buck me off or bite me. I have heard this stop has become a regular on the motorcyclist's trail through Africa after I first published a photo doing it.

I lead a fairly physical life, so I don't feel it's necessary for me to begin a workout routine before leaving on a long ride. However, if you are a desk jockey or weekend warrior, I suggest you prepare for your trip by getting into top physical shape. Consider taking a few long weekend rides to shake down your motorcycle and gear—and yourself.

Insurance requirements vary by country. You can find the specific requirement in travel guides or over the Internet. However, although some countries say they require an Inter-

HARLEY-DAVIDSON ADVENTURER DAVE BARR

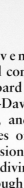

Dave Barr holds a Guinness World Record for his ride across Europe and Russia in winter on a Harley-Davidson. Before that, he circumnavigated the world, solo, on a Harley-Davidson, becoming the first person to do so. Today, he is an author, inspirational speaker, husband, and father. A double leg amputee (one leg off above the knee, the other below) this American adventurer still commutes aboard a Harley-Davidson, without a side-car, and is planning future adventures on his motorcycle. His other passion, besides his wife and child, is skydiving. I caught up with him long enough to hear his reflections on two-wheeled adventures with his Harley-Davidson.

Frazier: *You were lying in a bed in South Africa for a year after losing both legs to a land mine. What prompted you to plan a ride around the world by motorcycle?*

Barr: I had several goals in mind. First, I wanted to do it for people with disabilities, to show them and the world that a disability, especially like mine, does not need to be a barrier to success. Second, I wanted to be the first person to do a transversal of Africa on a Harley-Davidson. Third, I wanted to be the first person to ride a Harley-Davidson around the world.

Frazier: *What Harley-Davidson did you use to make your trip?*

Barr: I used what I had—a 1972 Wide Glide 1200. It had 150,000 miles on it to begin with, but I did have the engine freshly overhauled in South Africa before I started out. Sadly, I had to have the valves redone in Africa even before I got going. It was a real letdown to start out that way, but the South African guys who did the second valve job did it most professionally, spot on.

Frazier: *What was the length of your journey?*

Barr: When I finished three years and seven months later, in 1993, I had traveled over 83,000 miles on land with my Harley-Davidson.

Frazier: *How much did your trip cost, including shipping, repairs, food, sleeping, and gas?*

Barr: I spent approximately $28,000.

Frazier: *What was your worst experience?*

Barr: The motor going bad in Brazil. But then

there was getting pinned under the Harley on an icy road while trying to ride over the mountains to Ushuaia, at the tip of South America, and the avalanches in the Andes Mountains. And then there was getting pinned under the Harley in the sand of the Gobi Desert, and then... [Barr laughs]. Nah, the motor packing it in was about the worst.

Frazier: *What was your best experience?*

Barr: The people. Everywhere, meeting the people was the highlight of my trip, my best experience. Oh, there were great roads I rode, wonderful sights I saw, but the people made my trip.

Frazier: *What were your favorite countries or places you saw?*

Barr: China. I spent seven months riding through China, and was the first American to be in many places.

And Russia. In Russia I was amongst my sworn enemies as a [former] professional soldier. I actually met some Russians I had fought against. The Russians treated me with respect and kindness and I was given free rein to travel throughout their country.

Finally, there was Vietnam. I was the first motorcyclist to do both North and South Vietnam. It was fascinating, first to be there as an American; and second, on the Harley-Davidson. Whenever I had a problem it was someone that had been in the Viet Cong or the North Vietnamese Army that helped me out. I never paid a bribe and was always told, "Welcome back to Vietnam, GI."

Frazier: *What did you do with the Harley-Davidson after you were done with the trip?*

Barr: It is to be in The Harley-Davidson

Museum, along with some of the things I took with me on my ride. Also included may be the metal leg I had to have fabricated from parts from various countries and welded in a shop in Venezuela.

Frazier: *Do you have any tips you want to pass on to prospective motorcycle globe-trotters?*

Barr: Do not use a Shovelhead. I would take a Harley-Davidson 883 if I went out again. Also do not wait to find someone else to go with. Listen to your heart and do what feels best to your heart. Also remember that if you go alone you are far more likely to meet people. Alone, you yourself are far more amicable. For me the highpoint was meeting people, not just making and completing the ride. I would not have met as many fine people had I been with someone else.

it alone. I argue I am neither, but I accept that I am selfish in not wanting to share my adventure. Riding alone allows for greater freedom than riding with someone in tow or in front.

To make a long ride with another person requires that each party accept a certain degree of responsibility for the other, which is not necessary when going alone. To those of us who like riding solo, responsibility avoidance is a factor: when riding alone, the adventurer is responsible only for himself or herself.

Several summers ago, two acquaintances decided to ride to Alaska together. On the way up the Haul Road (the gravel section between Coldfoot and Deadhorse), one of them rode off the gravel and down a steep embankment. The net result: one broken leg, a helicopter ride back to Fairbanks, and a ride back for the bike in a pickup truck. The other rider visited his friend in the hospital, wished him well, and said, "Well, I have to get on with my vacation, so see you back in Denver." If it

had not been for the kindness of the local BMW dealer (George Rahn), the downed rider would have had to deal with getting his bike crated and himself back home. The two "riding buddies" aren't riding together anymore. In fact, they don't even speak to each other.

One winter, two BMW GS "Big Dog" riders from Colorado decided to ride together to the bottom of South America. In Peru, one suffered a broken collarbone from a crash. The injured rider wanted to ship himself and his bike back home. The unscathed rider wanted to leave the bikes, fly home, and then return in six weeks to finish their adventure when the collarbone healed. The injured writer, whose idea the trip was, won, and the adventure ended in Lima. Points were earned by his riding buddy because he had gone along as a wingman, accepted his responsibility, and did not abandon his leader. But by not choosing to go alone, his trip was ended by his partner's accident. Due to the cost and time involved, the uninjured rider

Headed to the "end of the earth," Ushuaia, Argentina, I made a day adventure riding "off-road" in unfenced and wide-open spaces, such as this field in Patagonia. In twelve hours, I saw not one other person.

A riding "pal" for several days taught me how to find cheap places to eat and sleep in his country, and how to make friends. He spoke no English and I spoke about twenty words he could understand, but both being "motorheads," we managed to communicate through our common interest in motorcycles.

probably will never get to see Ushuaia, at the southern tip of South America.

Another two riders decided to attempt a trip through Central and South America together. One crashed, breaking a leg in Central America. He was flown back to the United States while his buddy remained to ship the wrecked motorcycle back home. But the uninjured rider decided he did not want to take the rest of the trip alone, so he shipped back both bikes, then boarded a plane for home.

When riding with another person, having similar goals is important. Once, I hooked up with a female globe-trotter. She quickly learned how to ride a motorcycle, solicited a free one for her world ride, and flew her bike into New

York to start her global tour. A major goal of her trip was to get her picture published in as many newspapers and magazines as possible, and her voyage covered on television. In essence, she was taking an extended vacation and financing as much of it as she could through solicitations for money along her route. When we were in Japan, I wanted to ride the road reputed to be the best in that country. We found it one cold afternoon. She didn't want to ride the ten miles back to connect with it, and opted for a stay at a hotel and spa up the road. I agreed to meet her after I had bagged the "S-Train" road. Later, over dinner, I thought she would wonder about Japan's best motorcycling road, but she never did. Her discussion instead was about which magazines and editors she could contact when we arrived in Tokyo. Obviously, the purposes of our rides were in conflict. She wanted to be recognized while I wanted to ride roads.

Going alone means you ride to your own clock. If you want to leave at 4:00 a.m. to avoid the afternoon desert heat, you can be up and gone before the sun hits the sand, and you can stop when you have had enough. With a riding buddy, you have to come to a consensus about when to start and stop. This consensus also applies to stops for gas, food, bathroom breaks, repairs, tire changes, and sleeping. The time it takes to poll the other rider and come to a consensus cuts into your personal riding time.

A German friend, like me, prefers to go it alone. She has had solo rides across Russia (twice), from the top to the bottom of Africa, around the United States, and across Australia. While in the

Outback, she crashed and broke her collarbone. Since she had no one's schedule other than her own to worry about, she chose to stay put while the bones healed before finishing her ride around Oz. The downtime was six weeks; but during that time, she repaired her bike and made new friends.

There is no easy answer for those debating the options of solo versus tandem riding. The solo adventurer will tell you there is no other way to go. Group riders will argue that there's safety in numbers and that the fellowship of the shared ride is priceless. When I discuss these choices with fellow global adventurers like Dave Barr or Ted Simon, we cannot see ourselves going far in the company of another rider. The three of us also agree there is an immense personal satisfaction in completing a long solo ride. That satisfaction comes from knowing that we alone solved seemingly insurmountable problems, like the overweight motorcycle on its side in the middle of nowhere.

The Latin American Motorcycle Association greets me as I arrive in Cuba.

Dave Barr, a double leg amputee, would get his bike upright after unloading everything and using his scissor-jack to get it pointed skyward. After taking the strapped-on weight off first, I would rock the bike halfway upright using the cylinder head (the BMW) or the aluminum panniers (the KLR) to get it moving upward, then I'd muscle it the rest of the way with brute force.

Once the motorcycle is back on its feet and repacked, I can luxuriate in the satisfaction that I have solved another problem. Yet in a sense it is a shallow celebration because there is no one around who witnessed my achievement and can share in my sense of accomplishment. That is a price we pay, going it alone.

In response to my book *Riding South: Mexico, Central and South America by Motorcycle*, which recounted a solo trip over a six-month period, several readers offered suggestions on a variety of subjects. One reader thought I would have had more fun if I hadn't gone solo. Many of them thought I would have enjoyed the trip more if I had gone with fellow English-speaking riders with whom I could converse along the way.

The one fact that I have found to be true of solo riding is that I meet far more people, locals as well as fellow travelers, when I am alone. Local people are much quicker to approach me and offer their help when I am alone with my motorcycle, looking at a map or making repairs, than they are when there are two or more of us. I think they conclude that a solo person might need help whereas two or more can solve the problem themselves. I also think two or more traveling together are more threatening than one (whether physically or mentally) to someone wanting to offer help.

From a philosophical standpoint, when I look back on a long ride, the images of the places I have been, roads I have ridden, and sights I have seen dim. What remain bright are the memories of the people I have met. Many times those acquaintances have lasted for years; some are still ongoing. I feel many of them never would have been made had I been traveling with someone else.

CHAPTER
FIVE

WHAT
TO TAKE

There are certain items most riders should take and others I'd recommend taking. Then there's the stuff no one *needs* to take! My advice: do not take it if you don't absolutely need it or can't afford to lose it. A question travelers are often asked is, "How much did that watch cost?" Leave the Rolex at home and replace it with a cheap, functional watch. If it quits along the way, you can always buy another; if it is stolen while you are in a shower or sleeping, you have not lost much.

The Necessities

Often I'll find myself hundreds of miles from a town when my bike needs a repair. When this happens, I want a well-stocked kit so I can make the fix on the roadside rather than face a long walk. While I have used may different motorcycles, my basic travel kit remains about the same, except for spare parts for the specific bike, and special tools.

I carry a small tent and sleeping bag. These can vary in make, but most importantly, they should take up very little space. (When I'm carrying a sleeping bag, people more often invite me into their homes.)

Whether I carry cooking gear depends on the route. If I will be traveling in expensive countries, I add the gear. On a quick run across the United States, I opt for supermarkets and fast food. Cooking myself often costs more than restaurant food.

While making a long ride, I cut my meals down to two a day, foregoing a large breakfast. A soda or juice often carries me to noon and requires no preparation beyond buying it the night before. I keep some small food items, such as Power Bars, in my tank bag for snacks. Other necessities include travel documents, clothing, and personal items.

Documents and Paperwork

I make a copy of everything and keep all copies in a separate packet, well hidden. This precaution will help you avoid a lot of problems. For example, a copy of a lost passport can save you hours at an American embassy while they try to identify you. For security, I have a hidden pocket sewn to the inside of my jeans pant leg for valuables. I stash papers in and around the padding of my riding suit and boots. Everything is sealed in plastic bags for protection. It is a good idea to make color copies of your driver's license

---

PAPERWORK

The following documents are crucial for your trip:

- Original and copies of your motorcycle title and registration
- Passport and a copy
- International Certificate of Vaccination and a copy
- Insurance certificates and copies (Medical or travel insurance should include an evacuation clause.)
- International driving permit
- Driver's license and copies
- Expired passport (for leaving at hotel when going out)
- Debit card and two credit cards
- Cash (hidden in riding gear and on motorcycle)
- Traveler's checks
- Dummy wallet (with an insignificant amount of cash, expired credit cards, and miscellaneous paperwork; the contents inside should look real so if you're robbed, you'll have something to give the thief)
- Various letters of introduction
- Press credentials
- Several passport-size photos. These will be needed when you apply for visas along your route. It is often time-consuming and expensive to have them done while you wait.
- Address book and notebook for writing
- Guidebooks

This motorcyclist carries a versatile box of spares that includes old automobile parts. He had figured out how to adjust them to fit his bike.

and motorcycle registration and plasticize them. That way if it's humid or raining they won't get ruined when shown to inspectors. When police stop you for what may be more a road tax than a violation, they often keep your driver's license until you fork over the cash, sometimes telling you it can be picked up at a police station once you have paid (after you've gone to an ATM for the money). Consider letting them keep your duplicate and ride on out of the country.

Clothing and Personal Items

If you are going to countries where syringes and needles might be reused,

carry your own—sealed and protected—in your medical kit in case needed. I had my physician teach me to give myself an injection. To avoid questions by inspectors, I carry a letter from my doctor saying he prescribed them for my use.

A Few Additional Tips

Be sure you have a good contact (or several) who can send needed parts to you, anywhere on the globe. Do not accept your local dealer's assurance of, "Yeah, no problem, just give us a call or send us an e-mail and we'll send out what you need." Find out if the dealer has ever sent something to your planned destinations, if he is familiar with the customs forms, which shippers he uses, who the best person in the shop is to deal with, and how often the dealer checks his e-mail. E-mail proficiency is important because trying to find a telephone that works (for instance, in Siberia) during the hours your dealer is open can be frustrating and expensive. I once stood in line for more than an hour in 100-degree heat to use a telephone to call my dealer back in the United States for needed parts, only to end up talking to a trainee at the parts counter who did not know what DHL, FedEx, or UPS meant!

Trusted friends and family members can save you hundreds of dollars if they are educated about your bike, its parts, and shipping procedures before you leave. They should know to take any invoices out of parts boxes

My back wheel now sports a truck shock absorber, welded on outside the spring. Necessity being the blood, sweat, and tears of making do, I came up with this solution when a shock blew in Africa and there was no convenient motorcycle shop around.

they are sending you. They should know your preference for used versus new parts. Used parts often escape high import taxes applied to new parts when shipped into specific countries. For example, Brazil places an 80 percent import tax on new parts.

The Internet provides a huge safety net for twenty-first century travel-

CLOTHES

I pack the following clothing and riding gear:

- Gor-Tex jacket and pants (or similar material—I got rid of the leather stuff a long time ago, too heavy, bulky, hot, and not waterproof)
- Riding boots, preferably as close to waterproof as possible (I prefer Aerostich's Combat Touring Boots; they are bulky but have earned a permanent place on my gear list.)
- Rain suit, gloves, and boot covers
- Heated vest or jacket liner
- Heavy and light riding gloves (one pair each)
- Balaclava and scarf
- Full helmet with spare face shield

- Cotton socks, T-shirts, and shorts (enough of each for one week)
- Nylon swimsuit
- Heavy sweatshirt (long sleeve)
- Light sweatshirt (long sleeve)
- Jeans (one pair)
- Dress shirt
- Handkerchiefs (three)
- Lightweight desert boots or slip-on shoes for walking (one pair)
- Sandals or flip-flops for showers (one pair)
- House shoes (if going to countries where they are worn)
- Towel
- Belt

ers. The trick is to establish contacts before you leave on your trip so you won't be posting any "Help" messages to unknowns while you're away in a foreign county. Brand-specific bulletin boards and groups are the best source for locating people who can aid you.

The final element in my travel kit is mental—innovation. I once met a Honda rider whose alternator died while he was in Mexico. He parked and secured the bike, then hitched a ride back to the United States to purchase a replacement unit. When he returned to Mexico, he found his bike had been stripped. I mentioned that he could have purchased a 12-volt car battery, strapped it on the back, connected it with some wires, and charged it at night in gas stations and repair shops along the way. His response, "I never thought of that."

In Africa, my rear shock absorber blew its shaft seal. A replacement shock, shipped express air freight, was going to cost me $400, plus $100 shipping, possibly import tax, and at least one week of waiting time and maybe two. Instead, I visited the local automobile wrecking yard where I fortunately found a shock absorber the same length off a small Japanese truck. A hammer and a little welding got the shock affixed parallel to the blown shock, and for $5 and a couple of hours of work, I was on my way. While the repair was not pretty, it worked as well as the original, and it saved me hundreds of dollars and an unwanted delay. When I showed it to my local mechanic, he said, "Hmmmm, never would have thought of that."

I probably carry too much. When I rode my new Kawasaki around the world, I ordered a spare ignition module and coil. The Kawasaki representative assured me that I would not need a spare because the originals never go bad—and he was right. However, when I was in Ushuaia, Argentina, at Christmas and another motorcyclist needed a

PERSONAL ITEMS

I also bring the following odds and ends:

- Shaving kit
- Small double baggie with laundry soap (for washing things by hand at a campsite or in a hotel)
- Spare glasses
- Vitamins and prescription drugs (with copies of the prescriptions). In my travels, I've had to use: Cipro, mefloquine, chloroquine, TMP-SMX DS, penicillin, tetracycline, and various other over-the-counter items such as ibuprofen, Bufferin, cold tablets, and flu pills.
- Medical kit
- Syringe and needle
- Bug repellent
- Ziplock baggies
- Heavy-duty needle and thread
- Scissors
- Flask or small bottle of vodka
- Cameras and film (I do not bother with a tripod so I can take photos of myself as someone usually can be enlisted to take a picture, or a suitable rock or table can be found. I don't bother with binoculars either; I am a biker, not a birder.
- Umbrella (small)

TOOL KIT
AND SPARE PARTS

These are the general tools I carry:

- Standard motorcycle tool kit specific to the motorcycle I am using, replacing the "junk" tools often supplied by the manufacturer with better quality tools
- Complete set of sockets and ratchets with extensions; I keep these together in a plastic freezer box to reduce weight
- Complete set of combination open-end/box-end wrenches, from the smallest to the largest specific to the bike; at times I need one wrench from my standard kit and one from my aftermarket set.
- Long Phillips and flat head screwdrivers for those hard-to-reach screws
- Special pullers to replace the parts that typically break, like the rotor puller
- Multipurpose utility tool, such as a Leatherman; I keep it in my tank bag, for easy access, rather than in the tool kit under the seat or in the panniers
- Vice grips, both needle-nose and regular
- Adjustable wrench and file
- Small hammer or hatchet
- Hacksaw blade
- Two extra long and good quality tire irons
- Tire pressure gauge and flashlight

These are the general parts I carry; I add some that are bike specific:

- Inner tubes, front and rear. I recommend carrying tubes even if your motorcycle uses tubeless tires. A cut in the tubeless tire can be repaired by gluing a patch made from an old inner tube (or several, if the cut is large) to the inside of the tire. The tube can then be inserted and filled.
- Tire repair kit—the vulcanizing type. These repair kits use heat to melt the patch to the tube and are far superior to the rubber glue-type patches, especially if you are making the repair in the rain. For tubeless tires I carry a good aftermarket tire repair kit with plenty of plugs.
- Bicycle tire pump. Use the small two-way hand pump that pushes air on both the in- and out-stroke of the pump. It is about 12 inches long and can be purchased at better bicycle shops. I use this instead of the carbon dioxide (CO_2) cartridge kits because it is lighter. While neither pumps enough air to seat a tubeless tire, the hand pump usually inflates the tire enough that the bike can be pushed to a high-pressure pump. The CO_2 cartridges are often hard to find and expensive.
- Can of Instant Air. For a quick fix on a slow leak, this will get you enough air to ride a few miles to a gas station where a work-station can be found. I do not use this for anything other than a short ride because the gunk usually runs out of the hole in the tube or tire and makes a mess.
- Spare clutch, brake, and throttle cables
- Spare clutch and brake levers. Some of these are brand specific so there is little chance of finding one on the road that can be modified to fit your specific bike.
- Six feet of gas line. This has numerous uses, such as siphoning gas to the tank, filling the cooking stove from the gas tank, and replacing cracked gas lines.
- Spare clutch plates and springs. I do not carry a full set of springs and plates for multi-plate bikes; instead, I carry enough to solve a problem if some wear out.
- Spare carburetor parts, such as floats, diaphragms, and springs
- Spare alternator brushes
- Spare coil and ignition black box. On

This well-rusted bike caught my eye as I was passing by the vacant lot in India where it had been abandoned. In a country where few spares for motorcycles like mine could be found, this seemed like a good spare parts "store."

some of the new bikes, these black boxes are prohibitively expensive, so I try to use motorcycles that do not require the $1,500 electrical part and can be fixed without a technician and a computer. Some expensive parts I have purchased off of wrecked or "donor" bikes.

- A gasket kit. I use reusable oil and air filters so I don't have to carry spares.
- Brake pads, especially the front ones
- Headlight and taillight bulbs, especially if the bike takes an unusual bulb that would be hard to find along the way
- Fork seals and fuses
- Spark plug wire, caps, and spare plugs
- Repair manual, including a complete wiring diagram. This is not the owner's manual that comes with the motorcycle but a shop manual.

The miscellaneous items I carry:

- Bag of mixed nuts, bolts, screws, and washers for every item on my bike
- Hose clamps (small and large)
- JB Weld (KWIK). This material patches holes in aluminum, plastic, and steel.
- Shoe Goop. This glue is good for repairing everything from patches on tubes to rips in boots and tents.

- RTV gasket maker
- Black electrical tape and duct tape. Duct tape is bulky but has numerous uses, from lining rims to repairing broken turn signals and windscreens.
- Cable ties (various sizes)
- Jumper wire with alligator clips. This is not an automobile jumper cable (which is too bulky), but a small-gauge wire, sufficient enough for charging a motorcycle battery. I also connect them to a small 12-volt light for reading at night. My nightlight can also be used when I need to check electrical connections on the bike.
- Safety wire and electrical wire (several gauges and lengths)
- Electrical extension cord
- Small battery charger. A two-amp unit, will charge the battery overnight.
- Spare keys to all locks on the motorcycle, including security chains
- Rubber bands. I make these from old inner tubes and use several different sizes.
- Pieces of inner tube, 6 x 6 inch squares. These are good for many things, including tire patches, washers, and padding.
- Bead breaker for tubeless tires. Mine is big, heavy, and takes up too much space, but I have been thankful I had it enough times that I sacrifice the space and weight.

The best insurance against breakdown is thorough motorcycle preparation before your trip. Research the model of your motorcycle to understand its weaknesses; and, before you go, change what is known to break or die. Carry the removed parts as spares because even replacement parts are known to go bad.

Another couple of 'round-the-world trekkers get ready to travel on through India. They'd packed their bike carefully, knowing they would have to be as self-sufficient as possible when riding through countries with few safety nets for motorcyclists in need.

clutch plate, I had the only one for thousands of miles. I made his Christmas one he'll remember.

I no longer carry water filters or purifying paraphernalia. I have found bottled water in every country I've been to. When I am done with a bottle of water I often refill it with more bottled water that is available at hotels.

Rather than carry a full liter of oil for topping off my engine oil from time to time, I use a much smaller container, such as a shampoo bottle with a smaller spout. The smaller spout often makes it easier to squirt the oil into the engine oil opening rather than trying to find a funnel or making one. I refill the container at gas stations or from a liter oil bottle and then give the remaining portion of the oil away in order to save space.

If you are going to be riding where it is really hot and sultry, I recommend Kool Off Ties from Aerostich. These water absorbent kerchiefs are lightweight and take up no space when dry. Let one sit in water for a while (refrigerate at night) and they hold up to 400 times their weight in water. Worn around the neck they ooze coolness for

Learn how to change your own tires and tubes. If you don't have a spare tube or the hole in the tire is too big to repair, make a temporary fix by stuffing T-shirts inside the tire. At slow speeds this fix can get you to a town or repair place. If you have a tubeless tire with a hole too large to plug, try gluing a large square or two of an inner tube to the inside of the tire.

To make your helmet's face shield last longer, wipe it off with a cloth rag. Paper towels can scratch the plastic. If you need a new face shield and cannot find your make and model, buy a cheap replacement. Then cut a large opening in your old shield and glue the new one over the hole.

Pack a couple of pairs of latex gloves for roadside repairs on your motorcycle. You never know when they may come in handy. Once, when I was in Africa, I was glad I had them on when I tried to stop the flow of blood from a boy's leg with a compound fracture.

A flat tire has me temporarily spread out on the side of the road. Thanks to the spare parts I packed, I was back on the road in an hour.

a day or better. I also use mine as a headband when my helmet is off.

Make business cards or a larger printed paper with your name, home address, e-mail address, Web site, and some background information such as your goals for the long ride. Leave it blank on the backside to make trading addresses and leaving notes on the road easier than hunting for paper. I also carry some special cards that have a laminated photo on one side and my contact information on the other. These are nearly as good as gifts in many places. One of my friends has gone so far as to make stickers with the same information on them—a novel idea, albeit expensive if the quality is good.

Unique gifts from your home country are a nice way to thank your hosts for their hospitality. They should be small, such as pins from your motorcycle club. Gifts for village kids who flock to your motorcycle when you stop are a mistake. By giving them gifts you create an expectancy that the next traveler may not be able to meet.

What You Don't Need

When I travel the globe by motorcycle I usually go without a safety net, which means I am self-sufficient while on the road—no laptop computer, cell phone, or GPS. While the electronic gizmos are nice to play with, and some would argue necessary, I have managed four global rides without any of them.

Personally I find little enjoyment holed up in a stuffy hotel room or sitting in my tent at night, pecking out a

A global rider sees many wonders, such as this ancient monument in Laos.

diary entry on a laptop computer or e-mailing to lovers or friends. The world is covered by the Internet today: cybercafes are nearly everywhere. If I can't find one, there's usually a library, post office, copy center, or individual with a computer where I can make a connection. The laptop, for me, is just another valuable to worry about being lost or damaged.

As for the GPS, I find it helpful but not necessary. As one GPS supplier said, "They're like a CB radio. They are fun to play with, but you don't need them." Once I was traveling with a GPS addict in Nepal who stopped and shouted over to me, while looking at her GPS, "The border is right next to us." I looked, and sure enough, there was the border fence.

Of course, if you are going to carry a digital camera, a laptop is nice for downloading your photos, and the GPS can benefit from any maps stored in the computer. However, when I leave my hotel, motorcycle, or camping place for a stroll around town at night, I have less to worry about without them.

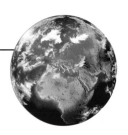

CHAPTER
SIX

WHERE
TO STAY

One of your earliest considerations should be whether your ride around the world will find you sleeping in a hotel, a tent, a hostel, or somewhere else. You may choose to do some of each. Factor your lifestyle, budget, and route into your decision.

With careful planning and the use of travel agents and the Internet, you can make reservations at hotels, motels, guesthouses, and hostels for the duration of your journey. Two years ago, I was planning a ride across Russia and using a travel agency to arrange my visa. After the agent secured my visa, I was surprised to learn he could book me into a hotel for every night of my trip. At the time, I was under the impression that parts of Russia were still outside the tourist paths. The agent informed me they had just booked another motorcyclist into hotels for every night of his ride across Russia. Since the bookings were in tourist hotels and each night was fairly expensive, I passed on the offer, but at least I now knew of the possibility.

I prefer inexpensive sleeping arrangements and when I cannot find them, I pitch my tent. I do this to spread out my funds, not necessarily because I like to camp. For example, I can pitch my tent in a modern camp in Germany for $12 a night, where I'd pay $60 for

This German guesthouse in the Black Forest drew me off the road for a night. Though not a Hilton or a Holiday Inn, it was only a quarter of the price, quite comfortable, and offered beautiful scenery.

a room in an economy hotel or $250 for first class at a Hilton.

Especially in expensive countries, I try to stay mainly in hostels or at campgrounds. This way, I meet more travelers like myself, ones who may be familiar with the roads ahead. While I have stayed in upscale hotels from time to time, I have seldom met anyone there who was knowledgeable about road conditions, accommodations, or meal locations. I will admit, however, that I get envious when I pass a Marriott Hotel and see several motorcycles in the parking lot because I know they are enjoying CNN and chocolate on their fluffy pillows!

I always carry camping equipment for those times when I travel in mild weather to places where no accom- modations are available. My camping equipment and motorcycle have never been turned away from a camp- ground, while I have been told, "Sorry, we're booked full," at hotels and motels. When a campground has been full, other motorcyclists have made room for me in their camping spaces. In the worst cases, I pitch my tent for the night in an out-of-sight- place, like behind a truck stop.

Several motorcycle marque asso- ciations offer their members books with the telephone numbers and addresses of people to call when help is needed; these books also indicate whether a spare room or workspace is available. In my travels around the world, I often used one of these direc- tories when an emergency occurred, such as needing to find a motorcycle part or a place to stay. People listed in these books are members of the associations, and they are listing their numbers for other members—not for outsiders who don't pay dues and support the organization. Unfortunately, sometimes the directories are abused by budget travelers who do not even bother to join the club. Instead, they borrow books from members so they can find free places to stay as they move around the world. Some have worked the system so well that they manage to get members in one city to e-mail or call ahead and arrange a place for them to stay at the next planned stop. Not much can be done about these abusers, other than making it clear that you are not one of them when you get in touch. Whenever I contact someone listed in one of these directories, I invite them to check with the association to confirm my membership and to get a reference from someone they might know.

I personally have learned the hard way to be wary of people who contact me for a place to stay after they get my name from a club's book. Once these budget travelers arrive, they like my workshop and accommodations so well that it's hard to get them to move on. Over a few beers, I sometimes learn they never joined the club and just got hold of the book from a member. They are, in fact, using it as a travel guide for free food and housing.

While I travel at the low-end of the budget scale, I do not abuse well-meaning organization members, nor do I condone those who do. At least join the organization you are exploiting!

DR. G'S "THREE-DAY RULE"

Staying with other people along your route is one way to cut costs. I have had many people offer me their homes, saving me hotel expenses. My hosts have also helped me sort out motorcycle problems, introduced me to their friends, and been gracious guides.

My hosts often say, "Stay as long as you like." However, I try to never stay longer than three days. Benjamin Franklin once said that "guests, like fish, begin to smell after three days." When I stay in other people's homes, my presence upsets their normal routines—just as I have found with guests in my home. Therefore, when I'm invited to stay with someone, I stay only for three days; then I move on.

Be sure that neither you nor anyone you send to hosts takes advantage of their generosity. I once helped another global rider as she circled South America by connecting her with friends who had housed me on my travels there. This freeloader knew a good thing when she saw it and maximized her stays at my friends' homes. She literally would move in for two to three weeks, using their houses as her "base." She knew the free meals and sleeping arrangements would ease the pressure on her budget, thereby allowing her a longer journey and more sightseeing in the area. In the end, her hosts always had to ask her to leave. The people I sent her to later wrote me and asked that I not to send my road friends to them again. One inconsiderate rider ruined the situation for everyone.

Camping Necessities

Long-distance motorcycle travel demands consideration for weight and space. Camping gear must be light and compact. The items you will need include a tent, sleeping bag, cooking equipment, and various odds and ends.

Tents

Tents are available in a wide range of style, price, and quality. I prefer a tent that is suspended from exterior aluminum poles because fiberglass poles are heavy and breakable. I also like a tent with a rain fly that allows for a large alcove or entryway. This lets me leave the wet and dirty gear in the alcove instead of dragging it into my sleeping area.

While a one-person tent packs smaller and is lighter, I prefer a larger tent because of the additional space it offers. Once I unload my gear from the motorcycle and store it in the tent, there is still room for my sleeping bag and me—very important! I like a tent with the highest dome possible. This allows me to dress inside in a near upright position or at least on my knees. With a smaller, one-man style tent, I have to lie on my back to get into my pants or riding gear, an uncomfortable exercise.

For the past several years, I have been using a North Face tent that sleeps two to three people; it's known for superior quality but has a high-end price. I have tried using cheaper tents—in the $40 to $60 range—and I still use them on occasion. I consider these throwaway tents; they're good for short-term use and when the weather is on your side. They usually pay for themselves in a week, considering the cost of a motel room, and after that, I figure I am getting free use. But, as they say, you get what you pay for. If I am using one of these throwaways, I always include a large plastic painter's drop cloth, or similar covering, to throw over the tent in case of rain. (I have yet to find a cheap tent that can keep out water for very long.)

Most tents come with a set of their own pegs; I throw these away and replace them with sturdier pegs. I try to find longer tent pegs made of aluminum, but I sometimes opt for heavy-duty plastic ones. The pegs sold with tents are normally short and soft, bending when hammered into hard ground and easily pulling out under strong winds. I always add a couple extra pegs to my kit to replace the ones that will inevitably get lost or broken while on the road.

I also carry a plastic ground cloth to place under the tent. Plastic takes up little space and the cloth keeps rain, dew, or other moisture from working its way into the tent from the bottom. It also extends the floor life of the tent. If the weather is nice, the ground is soft, or I am camping in the desert, I do not bother with the ground cloth. But if I suspect rain or see pointed objects like branches or rocks on the ground, I use it. I cut the ground cloth to the exact size of the base of the inner tent (not including the rain fly). If the ground cloth is cut too large, water can run down the rain fly, drop onto the ground cloth and get me and my sleeping bag wet from the underside of the tent.

American two-wheel globe-rompers Eric and Gail Hawes enjoy affordable accommodations and the friendly company of other adventurers in a campground in Belgium.

Before I leave on a trip, I set up my tent and stake it down to make sure that I have a complete set of pegs and poles and that nothing has been growing in it since the last time it was used. While it is up, I spray it with heavy-duty water repellent, open the doors and windows to air it out, and check the mosquito mesh for holes. Finally, I inspect the ground cloth and cut a new one if necessary.

I also check my patch kit. The kit supplied with the tent is good enough for a small rip or for one-time use. I usually replace the supplied kit with my own, made up of Shoe Goop and patches cut from an old tent or similar material. If my tent sustains a large tear or hole, I first sew it closed using the repair kit I carry in my luggage (a needle and dental floss can be used in a pinch), then cover my handiwork with Shoe Goop.

Sleeping Gear

With a sleeping bag, I consider space, weight, and price. I want the most compact and lightweight bag I can get, but it should keep me moderately warm. I have given up on the down-filled sleeping bag. While it has its pluses, I find it expensive to maintain and more expensive to purchase. I can get nearly the same amount of warmth from Hollofil or similar fill options.

I want a bag that occupies as little space as possible, can be cleaned in a standard washing machine (versus dry cleaning), is lined with nylon inside and out, and does not cost more than $100. If I cannot get the sleeping bag into a stuff sack that fits inside one of my panniers or saddlebags, I do not purchase it. Again, I view my sleeping bag from the standpoint of how long I expect to use it and where I am traveling with it. If I'm going to be camping in the snow (which I seldom do), then I want a bag with the lowest temperature rating I can find. On the other hand, I got around Africa quite nicely using a bag that cost me $25.

I like a bag that allows me to move around once I'm inside it; this rules out most mummy bags. At my height (6 feet 2 inches), I choose a sack that goes over my shoulders, and preferably my head, for cold-weather camping. For hot weather, I want a bag that unzips completely. (In Africa and parts of South America, I often unzipped the bag all the way and used it more like a pad than a bag.)

When I'm confronted with cold weather, a lighter bag means wearing more clothes while I sleep. When cold weather finds me with a warm-weather sleeping bag, I sleep wearing some riding gear and cover the bag with the rest of my gear, such as my Darien jacket and pants. (My standard riding gear includes a pair of long tights, similar to bicycle riding pants, and a long-sleeve jersey.) I usually wear a balaclava under my helmet. When I find myself in a cold climate, I wear the balaclava when I sleep, as the majority of body heat is lost from the head.

Another key to a warm and restful sleep is a pillow that keeps my head off the ground. Often the pillow is my rolled up riding jacket. I have tried carrying a little down pillow in a small stuff sack; it was a comfort at night but awkward to store. Now I use my Aerostich jacket (Kanetsu) liner which folds into its own pocket making a nice, but firm, pillow.

For thirty years I slept on the ground before being introduced to the wonder of self-inflating air mattresses. If the ground was hard, rocky, or cold, I would lay my riding gear and rain suit under my sleeping bag. I didn't carry a blow-up air mattress because of its weight and tendency to develop holes I couldn't patch. Then I tried a self-inflating mattress on a ride in Alaska. I was camping on permafrost,

I could have camped for free in this Cuban facility. I passed, however, since staying the night in a prison, even an abandoned one, seemed a bad idea.

ground so that the hardpan retains heat until well into the night, making it feel as if you're sleeping on a heated frying pan, the air mattress provides insulation that protects you from some of that heat.

Cooking Equipment

I limit my cooking equipment to the essentials. I carry a dual-fuel, single-burner cookstove that uses gasoline, which I transfer from my motorcycle gas tank by using the extra six feet of gas line I carry as a spare part. By using this type of cooker, I am not dependent upon fuel that is sometimes unavailable nor on propane bottles, which take up space and cost more than I like to spend on cooking fuel. The downsides to my dual-fuel cooker are the need to clean the jet more often (regular gasoline is dirtier), the necessity of storing the cooker upright when riding (to prevent spillage of excess gasoline from its storage tank), and the production of an ugly black smoke that collects on my cooking pan from the gasoline.

As for pots and pans, I carry a standard U.S. Army kit that you can purchase at most army-navy surplus stores for around five bucks. The kit usually comes with a self-locking handle, and is either steel or aluminum. I recommend the steel pots, which are easier to clean.

To stir and spear food, I use a small metal spoon, fork, and folding knife. For a flame, I use a plastic disposable lighter. For cleaning, I carry a small amount of liquid soap in a plastic dispenser, a brass or steel cleaning pad, and a dishrag. Everything can be contained inside the two pans of the army kit when folded together, and I store it

but my sleeping world changed! I now carry a self-inflating mattress when I have the space and add the optional cover and hardware that convert it into a recliner or chair.

I gave up valuable space when I added the self-inflator, but for me the trade-off between comfort and space was worthwhile. No longer do I wake up in the middle of the night with sore muscles or cold bones. The option of being able to turn the mattress into a chair has made evenings watching the sunset or sitting in front of the fire more enjoyable as well. I have also found it an ideal way to write or read when confined to the tent during inclement weather. An unexpected benefit of the air mattress is its insulating effect in extremely hot weather. I found it to be particularly helpful while I was traveling in Australia and Africa. When the sun bakes the

MOROCCO

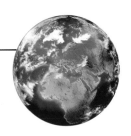

WHICH ROUTE TO TAKE

The route you take around the world depends upon several factors, including time, funds, and riding skill. The best way to plan a motorcycle trip is to determine how much time you have and how much money you can spend. Unless they have limited time schedules or are trying to set speed records, most travelers take between one and two years to circle the globe. This usually involves tagging the North American, European, and Asian continents while staying above the equator. It can be an easy route. If you follow only paved or sealed roads, it can be done in six months or less. But you may want to try difficult routes and travel over unsealed roads, for example, through Africa and South America. Then try to fit a route into those parameters.

Of all the continents, North America and Europe are the easiest to travel across because of the modern (paved, high-speed) road systems and ease in crossing borders. Next is South America. The most difficult regions are the Middle East and Asia. Not only are there paperwork requirements, but some borders are closed for overland travel to citizens of select countries.

Taking routes away from the big cities and off the beaten track can mean quieter and safer camping in places such as this one in South America. I simply pitched my tent and bedded down for the night in the Acama Desert in Chile.

South America

Traveling the South American continent adds time and expense to a global trip; it also includes a bit of off-pavement riding or at least some broken pavement. And, somehow, the rider must get to South America. Since there is no road from Panama to Colombia through the unpaved jungle of the Darien Gap (the only unfinished portion of the Pan-American Highway), you are faced with the option of transporting yourself and your motorcycle to South America by air or by boat, the less preferable option.

Some travelers choose to try and save a few dollars by shipping themselves and their motorcycles from Colon to either Venezuela or Colombia. The horror tales far exceed the success stories and include being dropped off on islands, learning that the boat is a smuggler's boat, suffering through days without food or water, and landing where there is no customs or immigration office to clear you or your motorcycle for entry into the country.

The smart travelers send their bikes over the Darien Gap by air cargo and themselves on passenger flights. Trying to save a few dollars going by private boat (no regular ferry service) is as foolish as trying to ride your motorcycle through the gap, now the main supply route for drug runners coming north.

Once you choose to add South America, your next decision is how much of the continent you want to see: north to south and east to west. Today, many riders fly their motorcycles from the United States to Ecuador because they don't want to ride through Colombia. Then they'll ride down the west coast of South America, following the Pan-American Highway. If they choose to go down the east coast, their option is to fly or ship into Venezuela, take the road to Manaus, and then take a boat down the Amazon. It is possible to ride into Brazil from the west coast, but road conditions, especially when wet, leave this option open only to serious and experienced off-road motorcyclists. The most frequently used route is the one by boat from

Manaus in Brazil to Belen. There you get back onto the pavement and head south through the country.

Africa

From South America, the choice is to go east or west, and again, it depends on time and money. The route east is the shortest if you go by plane or boat from Argentina or Brazil to Africa. However, this is an expensive option; it's also time-consuming and frustrating if you go by boat. Additionally, if you're going into South Africa, you need a Carnet de Passages (this is not needed in Central or South America). This is an internationally

In their encampment in Mozambique, members of a land mine cleanup squad inspect my bike. I was careful where I rode in that region; about once a week one of these guys would make a mistake and get blown up on the job.

recognized bond required to bring a motor vehicle into certain countries.

Upon arrival in South Africa, you are faced with more expensive and time-consuming decisions. For example, should you attempt a ride up the east coast of Africa or go as far north as you can along the west coast or through central Africa? Depending on the political climate of the countries, should you fly over countries that are closed to U.S. travelers, such as Angola? Border closings in Africa are dependent upon current political events, so you should be aware of such situations during your travels. I have been turned away from Algeria twice and also stopped at the border of Angola, but both countries allowed motorcycle travelers from Austria, Switzerland, and Germany.

Europe and Asia

The European continent is easily crossed and requires little more than time and money. You do not need a Carnet de Passages and nearly all the roads are paved or sealed. Food, gasoline, and sleep are easy, although they can be expensive in parts of Europe.

If you go south across Pakistan and India to Asia, you'll encounter some challenges crossing Bhutan. The government there does not allow solo travel by motorcyclists. You can make a detour north and cross China, but it is expensive and difficult because of the paperwork requirements. Most travelers get to India, then fly their motorcycles to points south, such as Australia, or to the east, such as to Thailand. A common route is going by air from Katmandu, Nepal, to Bangkok, Thailand. You can wander Southeast Asia, but you may be stopped at Vietnam or Indonesia. There's no consistency to the rules, however; some riders say they've been admitted while others were refused at the same borders. From Southeast Asia, you can proceed to Japan. Or you can go directly back to the United States. Another option is to fly from there to South America, then ride north.

The choice of a northern route across Russia presents some challenges of its own. You need to decide whether you want to try riding some sections of unpaved road, take the train, or load your motorcycle onto a truck. Some riders may opt to ride through a 500-mile section of swamp and logging roads known as the Zilov Gap, while others choose to load their motorcycles on trains and cross this section by rail, which takes three nights. In 2004, the Russian govern-

On a highway in Austria, I've stopped to thank the perfect skies that nothing has gone wrong with the multitude of gizmos on the BMW I am riding. Provided by Touratech for the European leg of my ride, the bike came with every available option the company could bolt on to a R1100 GS. It had some buttons and screens I never figured out how to use.

Mount Fuji as seen on a perfect day, along a perfect route, riding a perfect bike.

On the North Island of New Zealand, I've parked the motorcycle for a while so I can try some lake trout fishing. Fishing is one of New Zealand's many draws for me.

ment opened the gap road by completing the construction of numerous bridges across deep water crossings, making it possible to ride the Zilov Gap. However, much of the road is unpaved and under construction. It is a test for the pavement rider but doable, especially if you prefer riding roads over riding rails. Numerous unskilled gravel riders made the crossing in 2004. What might have taken a week to 10–14 days in 2002 could be easily done in five in 2004.

Australia and New Zealand

Australia is an option, but many travelers find it prohibitively expensive to fly their motorcycles there. The same is true with New Zealand. Both countries also require paperwork that is sometimes frustrating and troublesome. For instance, if you're traveling to New Zealand without a Carnet de Passages, you have to post a bond that ensures you will not sell or leave the motorcycle in New Zealand. The bond varies in cost from motorcycle to motorcycle. Be warned that it takes time for the bond to be returned to you once you exit the country with your motorcycle.

Australia is big. I spent six months riding around the perimeter of Australia; then, through the middle of the country; and, finally, into Tasmania. I was on the move during

TIPS FOR TRAVEL DIRECTIONS

Does a town have you so confused that you can't figure an easy way in or out of it? One solution is to hire a motorbike taxi for a small fee to lead you to where you want to go. This can save you hours of delay and frustration. The taxi driver often knows the shortcuts that are safer than the main streets shown on your map or GPS. Just make sure your leader knows where you want to go; don't depend on pointing to a location on your map because many people cannot read.

Getting good directions is often a best-two-out-of-three bet. In some countries a person will "lose face" if they cannot give you directions when asked, so they point and tell you to go one way—even though they have no idea where you want to go. If you need to ask for directions, ask three different people, then go with the consensus. However, if you know you want to go west, and two of those people are pointing east, go with the one who is pointing west—or ask three more people.

Learn to orient yourself to the four directions—north, south, east, and west. The sun comes up in the east, so facing east in the morning means north is to your left, south is to your right, and west is behind you. I once made the mistake of becoming dependent on a traveling companion's maps and GPS when we rode a long stretch of Asia together. He decided to turn around and go back to our beginning point in Germany, leaving me in Moscow with only a route map I had ripped out of an airline magazine, and a $1 plastic compass that a sponsor had given me as a joke. As I crossed the next seven time zones, I made several attempts to buy a map, but there were none to be had.

Since I stopped beside a speed limit sign right after entering France, I had no excuse for not knowing what it was later on. It's a wise idea to learn the rules of the road ahead of time for the countries through which you'll be traveling—if there are any!

most of those six months. While the daily travel costs—for food, gas, and sleep—were low, the cost to get there and back was high.

Other Routes

Some motorcyclists ride Antarctica—one managed to reach the South Pole, but only with a full support system. There is generally not much reason to tag that continent.

You may want to come up with a creative and unique route of your own or fit in a section of road less traveled. For example, some years ago Dave Barr wanted to ride across Russia, so he did it in the winter, when much of the Zilov Gap was frozen and he could use more than 200 miles of frozen river as a road. Ed Culbertson wanted to ride from North America to South America through the previously unridden Darien Gap. With the help of six bearers, he was able to carry his motorcycle through this 100-mile stretch and be the first man to make the north to south transition, truly a major accomplishment.

Neither my bike nor I like this much snow so I usually plan my route accordingly.

SHIPPING MOTORCYCLES AND FINDING SPONSORS

here is no one simple way to ship your motorcycle across the United States or around the globe. For the motorcyclist who wants to travel to a faraway destination and avoid the time needed to ride to and from that destination, shipping can be the component that makes the dream come true. On the other hand, it can be the component that turns your dream ride into an adventure in Hell. Remember, three-quarters of the earth is covered in water, so if you plan to make a world ride, you are going to have to fly or ship your motorcycle across water at some point, often at great expense and with much frustration. Even the most experienced global travelers do not have all the answers on how to get a bike across water.

As with shipping, there is no single, uncomplicated way to go about getting sponsors for your ride. Financial support for a ride around the world can take as much time to secure as the actual ride itself takes! Some travelers can pull together the funds needed in months. Others spend years putting all the parts together. I have had both experiences. Of course, it is nice when the ride, bike, and accessories are fully paid for. However, the time it takes to secure the sponsors often makes you ask yourself if it was really worth all the work.

It's best when dealing with shipping and sponsorship questions to arm yourself with as much information as possible.

Shipping Your Bike

I once rode my motorcycle across Russia to Vladivostok. After the trip, I contacted a Russian air cargo company at the airport about transporting my bike to Los Angeles. For a large amount of Russian rubles, I was told the size crate I needed and which day to deliver the crated motorcycle. I was then given an airway bill (stamped "paid") that assured me in writing that the crate would be in Los Angeles three days later. What the Russian air cargo company failed to tell me was it did not fly directly to Los Angeles, but rather to Seoul, Korea, where the company would handoff my crate to another air cargo carrier that would fly to Los Angeles. A week went by and no crate arrived. I called the telephone number on the airway bill but it turned out to be for a Vladivostok pizza restaurant! With no one speaking English in Vladivostok or Seoul, answers were slow in coming.

Here I am in Cuba faced with getting the motorcycle across water to the next land point. Every global rider deals with this often perplexing, time-consuming, and costly problem whenever he or she reaches the end of an island or continent.

Three weeks went by; then, the Russian air cargo company demanded an additional 25 percent be wired to a numbered account. When the motorcycle finally arrived in Los Angeles, a local freight company demanded still more funds from me before it would release the documents required to clear the motorcycle. Nearly four weeks passed before I got my bike back and the process involved several hundred people, including pizza restaurant employees, the U.S. and Russian embassies, several media sources, and at least five air cargo companies!

A European motorcyclist contracted an American freight company to ship his motorcycle by air to Seattle, Washington, for a ride down coastal Highway 1, the start of his dream ride. But handlers in the air cargo terminal in Germany misread the shipping label and loaded the bike on to a flight destined for Washington, D.C., where it landed several days before he was scheduled to depart for Seattle. The air cargo carrier in Washington, D.C., quickly contacted a freight forwarder who managed to get the crated bike onto a truck bound for Seattle and delivered to the air cargo terminal that was its original destination. The motorcycle arrived just hours before the motorcyclist did. He began his ride on Highway 1 unaware that his bike had made a solo journey across the United States on an 18-wheeler!

Another biker wanted to get his motorcycle from Portland, Oregon, to Daytona, Florida, a good three-day ride. Making that run in late February, a rider would expect snow, rain, and cold. Instead, the motorcyclist called an advertiser in a motorcycle maga-

SHIPPING CRATES

Mark your shipping crate THIS SIDE UP with arrows pointing up. One shipper turned the motorcycle crate on its side. While there was no battery, oil in the engine, or gas in the tank, there was oil in the transmission. When the owner collected his motorcycle he was surprised to find it out of the crate and well cleaned. The shipper noticed the oil in the transmission had run out all over the inside of the crate, so he discarded the crate and cleaned the motorcycle. The owner, not knowing this, refilled the engine with oil, installed a battery, and filled the gas tank. One hundred miles down the road, the transmission fried.

This is how small I had to make the motorcycle to get it out of Russia. The size was based on the dimensions of the door to the cargo plane.

zine and arranged for his bike to be picked up at his house and delivered to his motel in Daytona. He enjoyed Bike Week, cruising Main Street for seven days, then dropped his bike off at a trucking company on his way to the airport.

Shipping motorcycles, either across the United States or around the globe, is becoming a big business. This can be seen in the proliferation of advertisements in motorcycle magazines and by the services available on the Internet. Such companies offer door-to-door services; buy-and-ship services (fly in, buy your bike, ship it home); ship-and-tour services (ship your bike for use on a guided tour); and even global shipping. Ten years ago, there were only a handful of companies specializing in motorcycle shipping; now, there are closer to thirty operating in the United States alone.

Shipping within the borders of the United States is a relatively simple matter. It requires no more than proof of ownership for the vehicle and deciding whether or not to purchase insurance additional to that being offered by the shipper. Frequently, the motorcycle does not even need to be crated, and the shipping company will provide you with the pallet.

However, shipping outside of the United States can test your patience! Entry requirements for a vehicle vary from country to country. In addition, whether you ship your vehicle by boat or plane can result in wildly different requirements. Confusing the situation is the unreliable information offered by different agencies in each country.

CARNET DE PASSAGES

The one document that eases entry with all forms of shipping outside of the United States is the *Carnet de Passages en Douane*, or carnet for short. This is an internationally recognized bond administered by the Alliance Internationale de Tourisme (AIT) in Switzerland. The vehicle owner purchases it to ensure that the vehicle will not be sold or left in the country into which it is being shipped. While this document is relatively unheard of in the United States, it is standard throughout much of the world and is used widely by trucks transporting goods across international borders. Not all countries in the world require this document (I rode through all of North, Central, and South America without one), but in certain countries, like Egypt and Pakistan, it is mandatory. However, even in countries where it is not required, having it eases entry because many officials recognize it.

The carnet is not sold in the United States, but U.S. citizens can purchase it through the Canadian Automobile Association (1145 Hunt Club Road, Suite 200, Ottawa, Ontario, Canada K1V 0Y3, telephone 613-247-0117, fax 613-247-0118). Internet users can download an application from the Web site, http://www.caa.ca/e/travel/index.shtml. A carnet is not cheap. The bond itself is approximately $300, to which is added another $200 for "costs," some of which may be refunded when you send the executed carnet back after your return. Additionally, you will be required to place in deposit an amount that equals roughly three times the estimated value of your motorcycle. (An older-year motorcycle would require about $3,500.) The process for acquiring a carnet is slow and time-consuming and the funds you place in deposit will not earn interest. In addition, it is not unheard of to wait for more than six months after returning the completed carnet to the issuing agency for the deposited funds to be released.

For example, the tourist bureau of a country may give you one set of requirements while the agent at the customs office holding your motorcycle and papers may give you an entirely different set of requirements.

Shipping Advice

After crossing more than 200 borders, I have learned some things that make shipping motorcycles easier. Be prepared to pay more than what is quoted by the shipper, because there may be added costs unknown to them, such as entry and inspection fees, warehouse storage, and bond fees. As a general rule of thumb for shipping cargo anywhere in the world, expect to pay $2.25 per pound.

If you want your motorcycle to be where you will be when you get there, it's better to pay the extra money and fly the bike by air cargo. You do not always save money shipping by boat. The time spent on hotels, telephone calls, e-mail, and faxes as you try to find your bike may far exceed what you save on shipping. It is my experience that air cargo companies are more familiar with handling smaller packages—like motorcycles—than boats, which are more accustomed to handling 100 tons of iron ore or large sealed and numbered containers.

However, if you choose to ship by boat, you can save some money by placing your motorcycle into a container with several other bikes or even with a car or household goods. The cost of shipping a container, if spread across several people, can be more economical and the boats are used to handling such containers.

Since there was no ramp for me to ride up, dockworkers have to muscle my motorcycle onto the cargo ferry I am taking to Zanzibar for the next leg of my African journey. I had to pay ten dockworkers to lift it onto the boat on this side of the water, then ten others to get it off on the other side since the fully loaded bike weighed approximately 700 pounds.

If you ship your vehicle in a crate, try not to be too specific when listing the contents ("motorcycle" should be enough). Crates are often the target of theft and the crime is made easier if you list details such as "Harley-Davidson," "IBM laptop computer," or "Sony digital camera."

If you are making your own arrangements with the shipper, either by airline or boat, be prepared to pay cash, as many shipping companies do not accept credit cards. Find out which specific airline or ship your motorcycle will be on. You should also get the airway bill number from your forwarder or shipper. (When you ship, you should receive a copy of this form, also known as a bill of lading.) This is how you track your crate and motorcycle.

While it is ideal to have the motorcycle placed on your same flight, it rarely happens these days. Be flexible and plan on a few extra days of waiting time at your destination.

If your motorcycle is expensive, purchase additional insurance over what the shipper offers as its base insurance. This often requires the crating be done by the shipper or one of its designated agents instead of by you, costing an additional $150 to $500 for the crate. If you are building a crate for your motorcycle, make it as small as possible, because, usually, you are charged by weight or displacement (volume)—whichever is greater. Your crate should be built on a skid so a forklift can easily move it.

Freight forwarders are a must in many foreign countries. For example, you'll need an address to which you can ship your bike and a good freight forwarder can provide this. In addition, the forwarder will translate documents, secure signatures on required

On a Mekong riverbank, workers struggle to get a BMW onto a boat.

forms, and pay necessary service or handling fees (sometimes known as bribes) in order to move your paperwork through the maze of red tape. Shop around before committing to one forwarder or another. Prices vary, as do services, and cheapest is not always the best. Ask about insurance, storage of your crate until you return, and pallet costs. Find out how much it will cost to clear customs and if assistance is provided at the destination point. Do not be afraid to ask questions.

When dealing with the cargo company directly, try negotiating. For example, one American convinced an air cargo carrier to lower its price 25 percent by saying he had seen the lower figure on the Internet. (His bike arrived three weeks later than promised, which may have been the result of this ploy!)

The best cargo carriers are those with offices in the cities you're shipping from and to. Using an air cargo company with an office at your destination is different than using an agent, who may be little more than a freight forwarder and someone not employed directly by the cargo carrier.

Try to secure the names, telephone numbers, and e-mail addresses of persons you are dealing with at both ends of the process. The same information for their supervisors may be useful later.

Freight Forwarders

Dealing with freight forwarders can be murky business. With good luck, everything will flow perfectly. With bad luck, you will find your freight forwarder is nothing but a person with a business card and cell phone who uses a borrowed desk at the airport or shipping dock.

The problems with a freight forwarder can begin as soon as you contact the airline about shipping your bike. The airline may suggest a freight forwarder familiar with the paperwork requirements. While some of these forwarders adeptly move cargo all over the world, few have experience dealing with motorcycles, which is a very specialized business. However, freight forwarders aren't likely to say to you, "We do not want your business

WHAT SPONSORS WANT

I sat down with two adventure travel suppliers of motorcycle clothing and gear to hear their perpectives on the sponsorship relationship. Tim Bernard, of Happy Trails, and Andy Goldfine, of Aerostich/Riderwearhouse, shared their thoughts on what's expected from those who their companies sponsor.

Tim Bernard, Happy Trails

Frazier: *How do you prefer to be approached?*

Bernard: If the person seeking a sponsorship is well known (or assumes they are), then they can directly contact us with a brief description of what they want, product or money. Then we follow up with phone calls and written notes back and forth to lay the groundwork.

If the person is unknown (or perceived to be), the best way to approach us is by a letter of introduction from the editor of the magazine they claim will be publishing articles about them or their trip. If the person is a novice this can be trouble. They should offer to pay for the product and then be reimbursed after the article is published.

Frazier: *Do you like to see a hard-copy proposal for sponsorship or endorsement; and, if so, what should it include?*

Bernard: I have never done this. If it is over a certain amount of dollars I could see where this would be good. The main drawback is that we bring a third party of legal wisdom in and I think this would be a negative.

Frazier: *What is a good lead time for you to consider a "yes, no, or maybe" from a proposal?*

Bernard: Anything within 12 months for initial publishing is good. After 12 months could be bad due to market changes.

Frazier: *What do you expect from the sponsored rider in return for supplying them with sponsorship?*

Bernard: A classic mistake was [once] made by me not having our product name on the boxes we sponsored for a Kawasaki KLR. A competitor put his signage on my product. This is really tough to say what the guideline would be. Hindsight is great. I now make it clear what would be acceptable signage on my product. I would expect a good article that benefits both, meaning that if problems occur, the manufacturer has the opportunity to address it before being slammed. I would like them to keep me in mind for future articles. I would appreciate honesty and mentoring from the sponsored. I know the writer is basically a hired gun; I would just ask that they give [me] the time of day in the future or at least until high noon before they shoot me. I expect the sponsored to give me a date of publishing. This will allow me to ramp up production so I do not create angry customers with huge back orders. The power of the pen is mighty.

Frazier: *Any other comments on sponsoring riders for long rides?*
Bernard: I want to be associated with people of ethics and who are in this for the long haul. Everything I make is guaranteed to break! That might sound odd, but it is all made by man and used by man. We learn from our users. We have lots of customers but only a few that truly use the product to the point of destruction. Those are the ones I learn from. We live in an age where we can go to the moon and beyond and when we lose someone in the process we do not give up. We learn. Riders that ride are the testing grounds for those who have the desire but for whatever reason they cannot do the big ride. The occasional rider receives great benefits from those on the long journey.

Andy Goldfine, Aerostich/ Riderwearhouse

Goldfine: Because of the small size of our company and our very limited resources, we do not have any formal sponsorship application procedures. I am responsible for evaluating and arranging every sponsorship request, rally prize request, and all other "swag" and promotion related activities.

Frazier: *How do you prefer to be approached?*
Goldfine: A conventional letter or an e-mail is good because it is not an interruption like a telephone call. Following up by e-mail is convenient, so if a regular letter is sent, an e-mail reply address should be included.

Frazier: *Do you like to see a hard copy? What should it include?*
Goldfine: I'd like the request to be brief. First, the request itself; second, the mission or purpose involved; and, third, any specific benefit we might receive in

return. Brevity cannot be overdone.

Frazier: *What is a good lead time for you to consider a proposal?*
Goldfine: Obviously the more lead time, the better...but for the right opportunity we can be quick.

Frazier: *What do you expect from the sponsored in return for supplying them with sponsorship?*
Goldfine: Loyalty, honesty, humility, integrity, and being an excellent ambassador for motorcycling. I like having only a few long-term, quality sponsor relationships.

Frazier: *Any other comments on sponsoring riders for long rides?*
Goldfine: Because thousands of riders now routinely make long distance "adventure rides," these kinds of individual private trips seldom merit sponsorship. More recently, some adventure riders have associated themselves with a beneficial charity activity. This is admirable, but it typically does not affect a sponsorship decision.

Having foolishly tried to ride my motorcycle through deep water, I find myself paying the price. A long afternoon followed. Guess I should have shipped it!

because we don't have any experience with motorcycles. Here's the name of a more experienced agent." Instead, they'll take the job. And they do have something to offer.

First is a price savings. Freight forwarders receive a shipping rate from the airlines that is often well below what the consumer receives if dealing directly with the airline. This is a negotiated rate between the freight forwarder and the airline. For example, if the airline charges the consumer $1,500 to ship a motorcycle, the freight forwarder might get a rate of $800. These savings can be passed on to the consumer, in whole or in part, depending on the freight forwarder.

The second positive offering from a freight forwarder is familiarity with paperwork that is often in a foreign language. Depending on where you are shipping to or from, this paperwork maze can approach monumental pro-

portions. The directions may be in a foreign language, and you may have to fill out the documents in that same language. You'll quickly learn to appreciate a freight forwarder who knows the ropes—and the language—when it comes to forms and processes.

The third offering is help in clearing customs at both your departure and destination points. While many freight forwarders have offices in only one city, they usually can recommend another freight forwarder at your destination city who will help you through the process involved in getting your motorcycle cleared through customs.

Now to the downside of freight forwarders. In business, time is money and freight forwarders are in business to make money. Filling out forms takes time, so freight forwarders charge money. One freight forwarder could charge $50 to complete the Dangerous Goods form (motorcycles are commonly classified as dangerous goods) while another may charge as much as $200 for the same service. There is no set rate.

Some freight forwarders know which airlines carry dangerous goods and those airlines' requirements for doing so—such as no gas in the gas tank, the battery removed or disconnected, and no oil. Other forwarders have no clue about these restrictions, because they ship normal cargo and not dangerous goods. This ignorance can result in significant delays and problems. For example, one freight forwarder promised that my motorcycle would be on the next cargo flight out to my destination. Instead, it took nearly a week to arrive. I later found out that the air cargo carrier would only transport dangerous goods on every third flight, and no cargo would be taken at all if the airplane was not filled to capacity.

In another instance, a pilot chose not to carry any motorcycles on his flight after seeing several waiting to be loaded—a decision made solely at his discretion. This resulted in fifteen Harley-Davidsons being returned to the shipper's warehouse, where they sat for six days waiting for an accommodating pilot.

Rolling your motorcycle straight on to a cargo flight is sometimes an option. Other shippers require that the motorcycle be crated, with enough clearance underneath for a forklift. Still other carriers may only require the motorcycle be secured to a pallet. A freight forwarder not familiar with motorcycles usually recommends that a bike be crated, and this can be costly and time-consuming. While the freight forwarder may be able to suggest where you can take your motorcycle to be crated—usually at a cost between $200 and $500—the forwarder is not responsible for this step.

Once I dealt with an incompetent freight forwarder who initially told me that I did not need to have the motorcycle crated but needed only to leave it at his office and his company would transport it to the cargo flight. Upon arriving at his office, I was informed (by one of the "associates") that my motorcycle would have to be crated and that it would cost an additional $400. I figured out that what was really needed was for the motorcycle to be stored on something a forklift could get under so it could be moved around the warehouse and into the cargo hold of the airplane. I bought a pallet from a trucker, tied the motorcycle to it, and then covered it with my bike cover, all of which cost less than $25 and took less than half a day.

On another occasion, I realized the freight forwarder was charging me well above what it should cost to ship my motorcycle. I left his office, rode directly to the airport, and started talking with the air cargo carriers themselves. I was able to get my motorcycle "rolled onto" a cargo plane. All I had to do was remove the windshield, mirrors, and gas; disconnect the battery; and lash all the camping gear to the top of the seat. As a result, the cost to move the motorcycle over the Darien Gap in Panama went from $900 to $250 by simply bypassing the freight forwarder and dealing directly with the air carrier.

Generally, when using a freight forwarder, you have little, if any, recourse should something go wrong. Normally, you find yourself thousands of miles away from his office when you realize your motorcycle is "missing." At this stage, there is not much the freight forwarder can do about it nor is he likely to care. Once he turns the cargo over to the carrier and hands over the airway bill, his responsibility ceases.

Some companies advertise in motorcycle publications and on the Internet, claiming they can transport your motorcycle across the United States or around the world. Some of these are mere freight forwarders, while others are full-service companies offering everything from insurance (for your motorcycle while in transit and later, once you start riding at your destination), to pallets for shipping, ticketing services, and even complete motorcycle tour packages. While prices vary, these companies are generally competitive when it comes to the actual cost of shipping. Nearly all use airlines familiar with transporting motorcycles, and they are usually well versed in the necessary paperwork and customs requirements.

Sponsors

A globe-trotting friend and I were once trading secrets on how we secured some motorcycle parts for our travels. Both of us concluded that the amount of time and effort necessary to secure a particular part from a sponsor (in this case, a gas tank) did not equal the value of the part. We concluded that it would have been easier and more cost effective to have purchased the part.

Generally, sponsors want to see their product or contribution in ink or in a medium that targets their cus-

tomers. For instance, if sponsors agree to supply tires, they want to see photographs and write-ups about those tires in magazines read by purchasers of motorcycle tires.

The same is true with products such as cameras, film, and clothing. For the sponsors, helping the 'round-the-world rider is a form of advertising. For their contributions, they want to see the maximum returns possible for their products.

I have had several long conversations with sponsors and with travelers soliciting sponsorships. It's my experience that neither is saying or hearing the same thing. For instance, when a traveler asks for a product, he or she often will make wild promises about how much "press coverage" this trip is going to receive. Meanwhile, the sponsor hears "press" and it rings a bell in the advertising department. However, problems arise when the traveler is featured in a newspaper in New Zealand because that won't help a sponsor who only sells the product in the United States.

One unhappy sponsor found that he had been hustled by a traveler who promised wide media exposure for his product. In actuality, all the traveler did was post the logo of the sponsor on her Web site, figuring that would meet the sponsor's requirements. In the end, the sponsor felt, appropriately, that he had been ripped off. The traveler couldn't have cared less—she got the free product for very little effort.

Obviously, if a sponsor doesn't get what he expects, it leaves a bad taste in his advertising mouth when the next traveler approaches him with an idea or concept. I have found that what works best is securing guarantees from the media before I leave. I speak to editors of motorcycle magazines and travel magazines that may be interested in purchasing stories or writing product reviews. This assures the sponsor that there will be some ink, or media coverage, for his product; at the least, he does not have to depend on me to follow through with an article upon my return or from the road to receive the promised press coverage.

It's not an easy sales pitch, and like I mentioned before, hustlers or less competent solicitors have soured many sponsors. Over time, you'll establish a reputation for delivering and following through; this will make entering front doors of new sponsors easier because you can prove you have delivered in the past.

Several global travelers have found ways to market their trips through unusual means, such as raising money in the name of certain charities. While the ride may be for a worthy cause, the traveler still needs to make sure he can keep the public informed as to the disposition of funds raised; that is, how much is actually going to the charity and how much is being pocketed by the traveler himself. This is a tricky business—and a business it certainly is. Some travelers make sure the charity receives every single cent they raise through speaking engagements or solicitations, while others take the proceeds and move on, leaving contributors in the dark as to where or how the funds are to be distributed. If the organization receiving the funds notifies the contributors that money was received, it's good for everyone involved and keeps all of the parties happy. It also takes the burden off the traveler and ensures integrity in the process.

When he had to ship his expensive motorcycle, this traveler in Cuba wrote "Tractor Parts" on the outside of the sealed crate and the same on the custom papers, hoping to fool any would-be Harley owners.

CROSSING THE CRAZY WOMAN AGAIN— THE LAST MILES HOME

The Crazy Woman. When I cross her, I know I am less than three hours from home. Crazy Woman Creek originates in the southern tip of the Big Horn Mountain Range, and my home is in the northern tip. Sometimes when I cross the Crazy Woman the smell of the wind seems to change, becoming fresher, cleaner. It is as if I have stepped out of the rest of the world and into a bubble of translucence in the Big Horn Mountains.

As I ride my motorcycle the last miles home, I look down to see the Crazy Woman near the top of the banks; the water is dirt brown. To me the color of the high waters means that things are good.

In May we always need rain to bring out the lush green of the mountain grass and the bright yellow and purple of the spring flowers high in the mountains. A dry winter can delay the colors until June, which means we can expect forest fires. This year's high and muddy Crazy Woman means we might not have the raging fires that we had last summer when seemingly

America has some of the best riding scenery such as this view of the mountains near Moab, Utah.

half of Montana was an orange flame.

It is pleasant to arrive home on a cool, clear mountain morning. The motorcycle runs perfectly the last 500 miles, as if it knows the end of my trip is near and rest is waiting. I open my house after nine months to find it is as I have left it. The flowers are still on my kitchen table, now dried, the water has long since evaporated. The tape player starts as soon as I turn on the electricity, playing "Rocky Mountain High," the recording that was in it when I shut down the power late last summer. Even the notes I have scribbled to myself on a kitchen notepad, reminding me of last minute things to do before leaving, are still next to the stove. I cannot ignore my fishing pole and net, they draw me to my alarm clock and I set a 3:30 a.m. appointment with a cutthroat fish.

When I return from a global circumnavigation I make a campfire, put a steak on the grill, and reflect on where I have been since I left after that sacred one minute of solitude some months or years before. How did my trip differ from my imaginings of what was to come? This time, as the fire was burning several cedar logs down to steak-frying coals, I looked back on the last 18,000 miles and nearly nine months. In the flames I could almost see the bloody roads and carnage as I crossed India and Bangladesh, or the burning bodies wrapped in white cloth

on the Ganges River in Varanasi, where each morning they were cremating and it smelled like burning chicken. I reflected on the quiet sands of the desert of Rajasthan. The Indian-manufactured Enfield Bullet had transported me places I never imagined I would see, and numerous times it carried me to the tranquility a slow meditation ride brings.

Thinking about Thailand, I could still see the gold of the thousands of temples and the reds and oranges of the clothes worn by the Buddhist monks, as well as the lush green of the jungles. I would like to return to that part of the world someday. I'd explore more of Asia—avoiding the monster snakes as well as the little ones. My thoughts shifted from the snakes in Burma to Taiwan and the local people enjoying a snake meal. I smile, thinking of the fun I had with the 125cc Hartford and SYM as I rode around

A proud Harley rider poses with his motorcycle in a festive city square in Thailand. Thailand is one of the most colorful lands in the world to travel through.

This old, many-armed cactus in the Arizona desert is another sign that I am home once again in the USA.

humid, hot, and filled with some of the biggest snakes I had ever come close to. What a pleasant surprise riding the Amazonas motorcycle around South America had been.

Reflecting on riding the Indian Chief around North America, and later the Harley-Davidson, I remembered how easy and safe it was to ride long miles on our road system. As I rode around the world, both this time and the two times before, I saw more traffic police in North America than anywhere else on the globe. Passing out tickets in the United States is undoubtedly a major contributor to local governmental revenue and should be factored into our published GNP as a hidden industry. Both the Harley and the Indian escaped VASCAR, radar, and unmarked California patrol cars, due to the fact I had been trained over the previous months to ride more slowly on the 54-year-old Chief.

Finally, as the flames of the campfire died down, I thought about the friends I had visited or made along the way. While the sights, sounds, and colors of my ride around the world had started to dim, my memories of people remained vivid. I could still see the smiles of the children in Nepal who I let wear my motorcycle helmet and gloves. The glowing skin of beautiful women in South America floated in and out of my campfire, as did the faces of faraway Asian ladies. I recalled the fun I had with old friends I had not seen for a year or longer, some of whom I had met on earlier rides around the world. As I stirred the coals and placed the metal grill on the rocks, I decided it is not the things and

Taiwan—me a huge westerner on one of their little bikes.

Crossing Europe I had suffered my worst weather, the biting cold of the German and Austrian Alps. The BMW was fun to ride but without a fairing to deflect the wind and snow, I wore all the clothes I had with me, including several pairs of underwear, to keep from getting frostbite. Brazil was as I had thought it would be—tough, places I see as I ride around the globe that make my trips valuable, it is the people. I thought, "Yes, there are a few places I would like to go back to and visit again, but far more people I hope to see someday in the future."

Returning home from a ride around the world always brings a dark funk. When the trip is over, emptiness makes the beautiful Montana days of bright sun, green grass, flaming yellow and purple flowers, blue skies, white clouds, and red sunsets a dark gray, sometimes almost black.

While at home, I must use an entirely different set of survival skills from those necessary to survive day-to-day on the road. Instead of folding up my tent each morning and packing the motorcycle for a day of riding, often into the unknown, I start my day with a much-missed cup of American coffee and usually know what awaits me.

Not so when riding through the jungles of South America or Asia. Far different from dodging TATA trucks and buses trying to run me off the road in India, or people and animals wandering into my path as I crossed Bangladesh. No BMW or Mercedes cars doing 250 kilometers per hour as they rocketed by me on the autobahns of Germany or autostradas of Italy. Instead, once back home, I must contend with revenue-generating police, trying to take my money and driver's license away, or drivers in the left passing lane going 20 miles per hour slower than traffic in the slow lanes.

I know when the deep funk is on me, because this happened after my other world rides, so I tell myself,

Temples such as this one are what come readily to mind when I remember my travels in Bangladesh, a land of more than a million gods.

"You're just depressed because it is the end of a hard trip. That's natural, so shake it off and get on with the day." I was once told about a German man who, when he ended his long trip, could not shake off the funk. He committed suicide. I know what to avoid. It takes time to adjust to not using the travel survival tools I had come to feel were natural, and get accustomed once again to using my other set of tools, even though they may not seem to be as much fun. I remind myself that the home tool kit has brought me as much adventure and fun over the years as the road tools did around the world.

It is always interesting to find out what has changed since I left home, and more so this time because it was a quick trip. The short months I was away brought a change in our economy, higher gas prices, and a new political climate. I also learned of a friend's divorce and the death of my neighbor. I had predicted the divorce, almost wishing the husband his freedom quickly from a bad person.

The death of my neighbor, however, was unexpected. She always gave me a long hug before I left on a big trip and sincerely wished me a safe return. I liked her. She never wore a brassiere (said she "hated the things"), started drinking about ten o'clock in the morning, and rode her lawn mower over some of the grass around my little house while I was away. Her husband told me that just days after I left she had been diagnosed with cancer and that she died two weeks before I arrived home. It greatly saddened me to learn she was gone, because I did not say good-bye. I wanted to tell her how much I

liked her. I told her husband, and he said, "She knew." That day I was reminded I should tell my parents and brother how much I love them and how proud I am they are mine, something I always put off because I think I will do it the next time I see them. Usually, when I go off on one of these long rides, it is me who is expected not to be around at the end,

not those that stay at home and wish me safe travels when I depart.

Riding a motorcycle around the world can range from hard to easy. My trips are normally hard because I choose the more difficult routes, ride mostly alone, go places where Americans are often disliked, and prefer to ride trails less traveled. Others choose the kinder, gentler ride, opting to put their motorcycles on trucks, trains, or airplanes to go over or around difficult sections. Still others sign up for guided tours where GPS readings given out each morning tell them where they will find their reserved room in a four-star hotel for the night. My budget has never afforded me that kind of luxury, nor does it ever allow me to buy my way out of

Take the road less traveled—like the one that led me to this solitary, peaceful pier in Cuba.

trouble or across difficult borders. This last trip was done on a shoestring. Because I used different motorcycles on different continents, I never had to pay to fly or ship a motorcycle across oceans, thereby saving thousands of dollars. I slept in $2 hotels, shared rooms, used my sleeping bag, ate raw food from public markets, and was hosted by friends to further cut down on costs. Several of the motorcycles I used were uninsured. Sponsors and benefactors helped with clothes, motorcycles, equipment, and gas. My nine-month ride around the globe was done on less than $1,000 per month, including airfare to get me across oceans. Several times I experienced a great degree of stress and uncertainty because I had no Carnet de Passages. Three times I landed on a continent with no motorcycle waiting. I traveled with just my riding suit, my helmet, and what I could carry.

Someday I might like to try a guided tour or "luxo-ride." I might enjoy having someone else change my tire or fix my bike for me each night, getting their hands dirty instead of mine. Maybe I'd be in the hotel bar spouting tales of adventure to my traveling companions. I doubt it will happen, though, because I'm not willing to make a sacrifice—like selling one of my Indian Chiefs—to get the $20,000 needed for a guided tour. Nor do I think I would be very happy following a guide who would make my decisions daily, telling me which road I would ride, when I would stop for a meal, and when or where I could start and stop. Those that do take the soft rides are probably having as much of an adventure in their way as I do in mine; we just have a different sense of adventure.

One of my mentors asked me if I am now done traveling or if I had another trip around the world planned. I will travel again, but for now, I'm going to stay home and lick my wounds. I told him, "This two-wheel road dog is beat up and tired." Tired, and nearly broke, but not depressed. I have learned that the best way to cheer up is to immediately start planning for the next global trip when I ride over the Crazy Woman and that breath of fresh air hits me. The lesson of love and life I have learned from the winds on my motorcycle rides around the earth: never cross a crazy woman for the last time.

Riding the world can take a lot out you physically—but usually not this much (right)! If you're like me, you may feel weary when you reach home again but you'll also be filled with incredible memories of faraway lands and people. And you'll already be planning your next 'round-the-world ride.

RESOURCES

If you read just these books and visit only these Web sites, you will be set to make your long ride around the world. Anything beyond these sites and books is just added enjoyment before taking off on your journey around the globe.

Books

Aero Design and Manufacturing Company, Inc. *Lightweight Unsupported Motorcycle Travel for Terminal Cases*. Duluth, Minn., 2003. This book is from master traveler Andy Goldfine and his gang at Aero Designs. I especially like the "Useful Web sites and More Info" section. If you cannot find what you are looking for in this section, it is not out there.

Barr, Dave. *Riding the Edge*. San Diego, Calif., 1995. This book tells how a modern-day road warrior managed 83,000 miles around the world—the hard way—without the benefit of support vehicles, guides, and big budgets.

Liska, Danny. *Two Wheels to Adventure*. Niobrara, Neb., 1989. This book has long been out of print but is well worth the hunt to see how adventure riding was done when it was really an adventure and not just a long ride. It spurred my interest in long riding and global romps.

Scott, Chris. *Adventure Motorcycling Handbook*. England, 1997. What Chris didn't cover in his book, I tried to cover in mine. This is a "must read" for anyone planning a world ride. It gets a little dated, but Chris revises it periodically to keep things current.

Simon, Ted. *Jupiter's Travels*. Middlesex, England, 1979. This book has probably spawned more 'round-the-world rides than any other motorcycle travel publication. If you can get over the slanted view of an Englishman looking at the world, it gives a good taste of the world thirty to forty years ago.

Web sites

BMW Motorcycle Owners of America
www.bmwmoa.org
Even if you do not own a BMW motorcycle, this site has pages on global touring and contacts all over the globe. Joining several of its suggested mailing lists can get you answers from all over the world to questions about shipping.

Horizons Unlimited
www.horizonsunlimited.com
This is a site specifically designed for motorcycle global travelers by Grant and Susan Johnson. The Johnsons are seasoned global road warriors (twelve years on the road) who have shipped their BMW all over the world. Their site has a detailed section on carnets, a bulletin board for questions and answers, and a newsletter for subscribers. There is a detailed section on shipping motorcycles, complete with recommendations, horror stories, names, and contacts.

MicaPeak
www.micapeak.com/~marcl/pages/shipbike.html
This site offers experiences shared by motorcyclists who have shipped their motorcycles to destinations outside the United States.

Shipping Digest
www.shippingdigest.com
This site is good for shipping information in general (not motorcycle specific) and has plenty of links.

Aluminum Panniers Suppliers

Frank Doerr Truck Equipment
(412-488-8640)
www.Frankdoerr.com

Happy Trails Products
(800-444-8770)
www.happy-trail.com

Jesse Luggage Systems
(623-878-7113)
www.jesseluggage.com

Legend MFG
(360-210-4112)

Moto-Sport Panniers
(303-679-9316)
www.motosportpanniers.com

Rosel Import Ltd.
(888-ITALJET)
www.roselimportltd.com

Touratech USA
(800-491-2926)
www.touratech-usa.com